The Best of
Cooking
Pleasures
New Creations

Cooking Club
of
America®

Minnetonka, Minnesota

The Best of Cooking Pleasures
New Creations

Printed in 2007.

Tom Carpenter
Creative Director

Heather Koshiol
Managing Editor

Jennifer Weaverling
Production Editor

Greg Schwieters
Book Designer

Laura Holle
Senior Book Development Assistant

Stafford Photography
Commissioned Photography

On the cover: Pear, Parsnip and Leek Salad, page 40.
On page 1: Cornmeal Blini with Whole Blueberry Syrup, page 9.

6 7 8 9 10 11 / 12 11 10 09 08 07
©2003 Cooking Club of America
ISBN 10: 1-58159-193-4
ISBN 13: 978-1-58159-193-4

Cooking Club of America
12301 Whitewater Drive
Minnetonka, MN 55343
www.cookingclub.com

Table
of
Contents

Roasted Peaches with Gorgonzola, Toasted Almonds and Honey, page 19

Carrot, Cumin and Coriander Soup and Chive Rolls, page 29

Sweet Potato, Pork and Sage Pot Pie, page 101

Fresh Cranberry-Studded Bread Pudding, page 127

INTRODUCTION

The Best of Cooking Pleasures
New Creations

It's time to stock your recipe pantry with some *New Creations!*

Any good chef keeps a pantry stocked with cooking essentials — cooking's basic building block ingredients. Open this kitchen pantry and you'll find sweeteners, flours, raising agents, seeds, herbs, spices, seasonings, oils, vinegars, sauces and canned goods … all the elements that "keep" well and get used again and again. In the refrigerator, butter, eggs, milk and cheese could also be considered pantry essentials.

Each of us has a "recipe pantry" too — a collection of excellent, trusted, standby recipes that we love and have mastered, and rely upon regularly. Like a kitchen pantry, a recipe pantry is essential to our cooking success and enjoyment.

We need both kinds of pantries. But each does not stand alone.

To be useful, the kitchen pantry needs help in the form of fresh ingredients (vegetables, meats, fruits and fish), as well as specialty ingredients of many types.

Your recipe pantry can always use some friendly additions too. That's why we pulled together the best feature stories from *Cooking Pleasures* in 2002, and are proud to present all the recipes to you in *The Best of Cooking Pleasures — New Creations*.

Here are ideas and inspirations for new cooking adventures you will want to take … "ingredients" to add to your recipe pantry. We hope you love these recipes, all organized and presented in one convenient, commemorative and beautiful book. Because while the basics are important, it is the *New Creations* that add extra excitement and joy to your cooking life.

Roasted Game Hens with Apricot-Mustard Glaze, page 63

Baked Feta with Sweet and Hot Peppers, page 23

Beef and Root Vegetable Pot Pie, page 102

Fluted Strawberry-Rhubarb Tarts, page 115

Strawberry-Walnut Salad with Warm Goat Cheese

Goat Cheese with Macadamia Nuts and Fresh Berries

Mediterranean Roast Chicken with Goat Cheese Stuffing

Roasted Peaches with Gorgonzola, Toasted Almonds and Honey

Starters & Appetizers Starters & Appetizers

Starters & Appetizers Starters & Appetizers

Starters & Appetizers

Starters & Appetizers Starters & Appetizers

Starters & Appetizers Starters & Appetizers

Baked Feta with Sweet and Hot Peppers

Cornmeal Blini with Whole Blueberry Syrup

Blini for Brunch

Classic Russian fare takes a sweet turn to become a morning star.

Text and Recipes by Jill Van Cleave

Americans love their pancakes. Hot off the griddle and doused in syrup, they're a breakfast staple throughout the year, especially during the holidays. This season, treat your family and friends to the Russian version of pancakes — blini. Small and yeast-risen, they're traditionally topped with sour cream or caviar and served as hors d'oeuvres. But they also make a delicious foundation for fruit and syrup.

In addition to containing yeast, blini typically are made with buckwheat flour. It gives them an earthy color and has its own distinctively tart taste. But blini can be made with other grains, too, such as cornmeal and whole wheat flour. Cornmeal lends a sunny color and slightly sweet flavor, while whole wheat flour gives blini a nutty taste. Although blini batter is thicker than pancake batter, it produces light-textured, puffy cakes.

For busy holiday cooks, blini have the edge on convenience over traditional pancakes. The batter is prepared ahead and refrigerated overnight. Syrups and sauces also can be made in advance, and cooked blini can be held in a warm oven for up to 30 minutes before serving.

Mix up a batch and start a new holiday tradition — blini for brunch.

Cornmeal Blini

Beaten egg whites folded into blini batter just before cooking result in heavenly, featherweight cakes. Use stone-ground cornmeal to provide a pleasant, slightly crunchy texture. Serve these with Whole Blueberry Syrup.

- 1 cup all-purpose flour
- 1 cup yellow cornmeal
- 1/4 cup sugar
- 1 teaspoon active dry yeast
- 1/4 heaping teaspoon salt
- 2 cups low-fat buttermilk
- 6 tablespoons unsalted butter, cut up
- 3 eggs, separated

1 In large bowl, whisk together flour, cornmeal, sugar, yeast and salt.
2 In small saucepan, carefully heat buttermilk and butter over medium heat just until butter begins to melt. (If mixture gets too hot, buttermilk will curdle.) Remove from heat; stir until butter is melted. Whisk into flour mixture. Add egg yolks; whisk until batter is completely smooth. Cover and refrigerate egg whites. Cover batter with plastic wrap.
3 Let stand at room temperature 1 hour or until mixture has nearly doubled in size and is bubbly. Stir batter down; cover and refrigerate overnight.
4 Remove batter and egg whites from refrigerator; let stand 30 minutes or until room temperature. In large bowl, beat egg whites at medium-high speed until stiff peaks form; fold into batter.
5 Heat griddle or nonstick skillet over medium heat until hot; lightly grease surface. For each pancake, pour scant 1/4 cup batter onto hot griddle. Cook 1 1/2 to 2 minutes or until puffed and bubbly throughout with slightly dry edges. Turn cakes; cook 30 to 60 seconds or until lightly browned.
6 Stack blini on baking sheet lined with paper towels; cover loosely with paper towel and foil. To keep warm, place in 175°F. oven for up to 30 minutes. Serve warm with Whole Blueberry Syrup.
About 25 (4-inch) pancakes

PER PANCAKE: 90 calories, 4 g total fat (2 g saturated fat), 2.5 g protein, 11 g carbohydrate, 35 mg cholesterol, 45 mg sodium, .5 g fiber

Whole Blueberry Syrup

Barely cooked whole blueberries float in this breakfast syrup sweetened with honey and brown sugar. Pair the syrup with Cornmeal Blini *and serve with ham or smoky bacon slices.*

- 1/3 cup unsalted butter
- 1/2 cup packed light brown sugar
- 1/4 cup honey
- 2 tablespoons water
- 1/4 teaspoon ground nutmeg
- 1 1/2 cups fresh blueberries

1 In medium saucepan, combine butter, brown sugar and honey. Bring to a boil over medium heat, stirring occasionally. Stir in water. Bring to a boil; boil 2 minutes.
2 Add nutmeg and blueberries. Cook, stirring occasionally, until mixture returns to a boil. Remove from heat. (Syrup can be made up to 24 hours ahead. Cover and refrigerate.) Serve barely warm or at room temperature.
1 2/3 cups

PER 2 TABLESPOONS: 105 calories, 5 g total fat (3 g saturated fat), 0 g protein, 16 g carbohydrate, 15 mg cholesterol, 5 mg sodium, .5 g fiber

Whole Wheat Blini

These blini most resemble American-style pancakes but have a lighter texture and quiet flavor, one that welcomes toppings and sauces, both sweet and savory. Serve these blini with Roasted Banana-Caramel Sauce.

- 1 cup all-purpose flour
- 1 cup whole wheat flour
- 2 tablespoons sugar
- 1/2 teaspoon active dry yeast
- 1/2 teaspoon salt
- 1 teaspoon cinnamon
- 1/4 teaspoon nutmeg
- 2 cups whole milk
- 6 tablespoons unsalted butter, cut up
- 2 eggs, room temperature, lightly beaten

1 In large bowl, whisk together all-purpose flour, whole wheat flour, sugar, yeast, salt, cinnamon and nutmeg.

2 In small saucepan, heat milk and butter over medium heat until butter just begins to melt. Remove from heat; stir until melted. Whisk into flour mixture. Add eggs; whisk until batter is completely smooth. Cover with plastic wrap.

3 Let stand at room temperature 1 hour or until mixture has nearly doubled in size and is bubbly. Stir batter down; cover and refrigerate overnight.

4 Remove batter from refrigerator; let stand 30 minutes or until room temperature.

5 Heat griddle or nonstick skillet over medium heat until hot; lightly grease surface. For each pancake, pour scant 1/4 cup batter onto hot griddle. Cook 1 to 1 1/2 minutes or until puffed and bubbly throughout with slightly dry edges. Turn cakes; cook 30 to 60 seconds or until lightly browned.

6 Stack blini on baking sheet lined with paper towels; cover loosely with paper towel and foil. To keep warm, place in 175°F. oven for up to 30 minutes. Serve warm with Roasted Banana-Caramel Sauce.

About 24 (4-inch) pancakes

PER PANCAKE: 85 calories, 4.5 g total fat (2.5 g saturated fat), 2.5 g protein, 10 g carbohydrate, 30 mg cholesterol, 65 mg sodium, 1 g fiber

Buttermilk Buckwheat Blini

Pair these light, airy cakes with Lemon Syrup, *or serve them with their traditional partners, salmon and sour cream.*

- 1 cup buckwheat flour
- 1 cup all-purpose flour
- 3 tablespoons sugar
- 1 teaspoon active dry yeast
- 1/2 teaspoon salt
- 2 cups low-fat buttermilk
- 6 tablespoons unsalted butter, cut up
- 3 large eggs, room temperature, lightly beaten*

1 In large bowl, stir together buckwheat flour, all-purpose flour, sugar, yeast and salt.

2 In small saucepan, carefully heat buttermilk and butter over medium heat just until butter begins to melt. (If mixture gets too hot, buttermilk will curdle.) Remove from heat; stir until butter is melted. Whisk into flour mixture. Add eggs; whisk until batter is completely smooth. Cover with plastic wrap.

3 Let stand at room temperature 1 hour or until mixture has nearly doubled in size and is bubbly. Stir batter down; cover and refrigerate overnight.

4 Remove batter from refrigerator; let stand 30 minutes or until room temperature.

5 Heat griddle or nonstick skillet over medium heat until hot; lightly grease surface. For each pancake, pour scant 1/4 cup batter onto hot griddle. Cook 1 to 1 1/2 minutes or until puffed with slightly dry edges. Turn cakes; cook an additional 1 to 1 1/2 minutes or until lightly browned.

6 Stack blini on baking sheet lined with paper towels; cover loosely with paper towel and foil. To keep warm, place in 175°F. oven for up to 30 minutes. Serve warm blini with Lemon Syrup.

TIP *To bring eggs to room temperature, place whole eggs in bowl of hot water 10 to 15 minutes.

About 25 (4-inch) pancakes

PER PANCAKE: 85 calories, 4 g total fat (2 g saturated fat), 2.5 g protein, 10 g carbohydrate, 35 mg cholesterol, 65 mg sodium, .5 g fiber

Lemon Syrup

This sweet-tart lemony syrup is both light and refreshing. The addition of butter eliminates the need for spreading more of it on the blini.

- 1/2 cup sugar
- 1 tablespoon cornstarch
- 1/8 teaspoon ground cardamom
- 1 cup water
- 2 tablespoons butter
- 1 teaspoon grated lemon peel
- 2 tablespoons fresh lemon juice

1 In small saucepan, stir together sugar, cornstarch and cardamom; whisk in water. Cook over medium heat 4 to 5 minutes or until mixture is thick and clear, stirring occasionally.

2 Add butter, lemon peel and lemon juice, stirring just until butter melts. Remove from heat. (Syrup can be made up to 3 days ahead. Cover and refrigerate. Reheat before serving.)

1 1/3 cups

PER 2 TABLESPOONS: 65 calories, 2.5 g total fat (1.5 g saturated fat), 0 g protein, 11 g carbohydrate, 6 mg cholesterol, 16.5 mg sodium, 0 g fiber

Blini Batter

The yeast-leavened blini batter should be prepared ahead and refrigerated overnight. Mix the batter in a very large bowl because it will rise considerably during the night. After the batter has doubled in size and is bubbly, it's ready to be stirred down, covered and refrigerated.

Roasted Banana-Caramel Sauce

Roasting bananas intensifies their flavor and is particularly useful for not-quite-ripe fruit. The resulting puree lends a deliciously different taste dimension to sweet, creamy caramel and additionally thickens the sauce.

  1 medium banana, unpeeled
  ¾ cup pecan halves
  ¼ cup water
  1 cup sugar
  1 cup heavy whipping cream, room temperature
  ¼ teaspoon vanilla

1 Heat oven to 350°F. Place banana on baking sheet; bake 20 minutes or until skin blackens and pulp is soft, turning once.

2 Meanwhile, place pecans on small rimmed baking sheet. Bake in same oven with banana 8 to 10 minutes or until fragrant and light brown.

3 Let banana stand 10 minutes or until cool enough to handle. Peel; remove soft pulp. (Banana can be prepared up to 1 day ahead. Cover and refrigerate pulp.) Place pulp on plate; mash with fork until smooth.

4 Meanwhile, place water in heavy medium saucepan; add sugar. Bring to a boil over medium heat, swirling pan frequently and brushing edges of pan with water to remove sugar. Boil 18 to 22 minutes or until sugar turns deep golden brown, swirling pan once or twice.

5 Remove pan from heat; add cream, stirring with long-handled wooden spoon (be careful as mixture will bubble up and spatter).

6 Place pan on medium-low heat; stir constantly until hardened caramel dissolves. Stir in banana puree and vanilla; cool slightly. Place in blender or food processor; process until smooth. Serve warm with blini; garnish with toasted pecans. (Sauce can be made up to 1 day ahead. Cover and refrigerate. Reheat before serving.)

2 cups

PER 2 TABLESPOONS: 135 calories, 8 g total fat (3 g saturated fat), 1 g protein, 15.5 g carbohydrate, 15 mg cholesterol, 5 mg sodium, .5 g fiber

Jill Van Cleave is a food writer and cookbook author based in Chicago. She is the author of *The Neighborhood Bake Shop* (William Morrow & Co.).

Strawberry-Walnut Salad with Warm Goat Cheese

Say Goat Cheese

From pasta to pastries, it brings distinctive tastes & textures to cooking.

Recipes by Hallie Harron

Its days of obscurity are over. Goat cheese has gone mainstream, and that's a boon to cooks everywhere. Thanks to local producers making it more readily available, and a wider variety of flavors and textures from which to choose, goat cheese now carries ingredient status.

Not long ago, most goat cheese was imported from Europe and available only in large markets. But in the last few years, dozens of small U.S. dairies have begun to produce award-winning cheeses. As production has increased, so has availability and selection. Today, American goat cheese is in most grocery stores, along with many European varieties.

If you haven't cooked with goat cheese, now's your chance. From a crunchy appetizer to a creamy cheesecake, these dishes will help you two get better acquainted.

Strawberry-Walnut Salad with Warm Goat Cheese

To get the most kudos at a dinner party, toast the walnuts while the cheese heats and serve both warm. This is truly a sublime marriage!

SALAD
- 2 tablespoons chopped toasted walnuts, ground*
- 4 oz. ash-ripened or plain goat cheese log, cut crosswise into 4 pieces
- 4 cups slightly packed torn Boston or Bibb lettuce
- 1½ cups halved small strawberries
- ½ cup toasted walnut halves*

VINAIGRETTE
- ¼ cup extra-virgin olive oil
- 2 tablespoons lemon juice
- 1 teaspoon walnut oil
- 1 tablespoon minced Italian parsley
- 1 tablespoon grated lemon peel
- ¼ teaspoon salt
- ⅛ teaspoon freshly ground pepper

1 Heat oven to 375°F. Line baking sheet with parchment paper. Place ground walnuts in shallow bowl. Press edges of cheese rounds into nuts, coating all sides. Place on baking sheet; refrigerate until right before serving.

2 In medium bowl, whisk together all vinaigrette ingredients.

3 Immediately before serving, bake cheese 5 minutes or until warm and slightly soft. (Cheese should be warm but still hold its shape.)

4 Meanwhile, in large bowl, toss lettuce with enough vinaigrette to lightly coat. Place on serving platter or individual salad plates. Arrange strawberries and walnut halves around plate over salad. Place cheese rounds on top of salad. Serve immediately.

TIP *To toast walnuts, spread on baking sheet; bake at 375°F. for 7 to 10 minutes or until lightly browned. Cool. To grind, place in food processor; pulse until finely ground.

4 servings

PER SERVING: 330 calories, 30.5 g total fat (7 g saturated fat), 7 g protein, 10 g carbohydrate, 25 mg cholesterol, 250 mg sodium, 3 g fiber

Crispy Goat Cheese Turnovers

A mild, soft goat cheese can add the same richness as cream cheese but with a distinctive, slightly tangy flavor that's actually lower in fat. These turnovers can be baked ahead and frozen for those unexpected tea time or cocktail guests. To reheat, bake the frozen turnovers on a baking sheet at 350°F. for 6 to 8 minutes.

DOUGH
- 1 cup all-purpose flour
- 2 teaspoons baking powder
- ¼ teaspoon sea salt
- ¼ teaspoon freshly ground pepper
- 4 oz. mild soft goat cheese, softened
- ½ cup unsalted butter, softened

FILLING
- 4 oz. herb-coated mild soft goat cheese
- 3 medium green onions, minced
- 1 egg
- ½ cup (2 oz.) shredded goat cheddar cheese, divided
- Dash salt

EGG WASH
- 1 egg, lightly beaten

1 In large bowl, stir together flour, baking powder, salt and pepper. Add 4 oz. mild goat cheese and butter. Using electric mixer fitted with paddle, beat at medium speed until soft dough forms. (Or use fingertips or pastry blender to blend dough ingredients.) Shape dough into ¾-inch-thick round. Wrap in plastic wrap; refrigerate 1 hour.

2 Meanwhile, in medium bowl, mix together all filling ingredients except ¼ cup of the shredded cheese.

3 On floured surface, roll dough ⅛ inch thick. Using 2¾-inch biscuit cutter, cut out 26 rounds, rerolling dough scraps if necessary. Place 1 heaping teaspoon filling on bottom half of each round; fold top half of dough over filling to form turnover. Crimp edges with fork. Place on baking sheet; cover and refrigerate at least 1 hour or overnight.

4 Heat oven to 375°F. Line another baking sheet with parchment paper; place turnovers on baking sheet. Brush each with egg wash. Bake 10 minutes. Sprinkle turnovers with reserved cheddar cheese. Bake an additional 5 to 10 minutes or until light brown. (Tops will appear somewhat blistered.) Cool 5 minutes; serve warm.

26 turnovers

PER TURNOVER: 85 calories, 6.5 g total fat (4 g saturated fat), 3 g protein, 4.5 g carbohydrate, 35 mg cholesterol, 115 mg sodium, 0 g fiber

Creamy Goat Cheese Pasta with Shrimp

The pungent aged goat cheese is a great foil for the delicate shrimp. Serve this dish as a first course or as a main course, with a salad and crusty bread.

SHRIMP
2 tablespoons extra-virgin olive oil
1 tablespoon lemon juice
2 tablespoons minced fresh chives
¼ teaspoon sea salt
¼ teaspoon freshly ground pepper
1 lb. shelled, deveined uncooked medium shrimp

SAUCE
1 (7-oz.) jar roasted red bell peppers, drained
1¼ cups heavy cream
2 teaspoons grated lemon peel
⅛ teaspoon ground white pepper

PASTA
12 oz. fettuccine
1 cup (4 oz.) aged goat cheese, shredded
1 lemon, cut into 6 thin wedges

1 In medium bowl, combine all shrimp ingredients. Cover and refrigerate 1 to 3 hours, stirring occasionally to coat shrimp on all sides. Meanwhile, in food processor or blender, puree bell peppers until smooth.

2 Cook fettuccine in lightly salted water according to package directions. Meanwhile, place shrimp with marinade in large skillet over high heat. Cook 2 to 3 minutes or until shrimp turn pink, turning once.

3 Remove shrimp, leaving excess liquid in skillet. Add cream, lemon peel and white pepper. Bring to a boil over high heat. Boil 3 to 4 minutes or until slightly thickened. Stir in shrimp and pepper puree.

4 Drain pasta but do not shake all liquid from noodles. Toss pasta with sauce. Sprinkle with goat cheese; garnish with lemon wedges.

WINE This very rich pasta needs a white wine with similar weight. Concha y Toro "Casillero del Diablo" Sauvignon Blanc from Chile is a great value. Or try the Mason Sauvignon Blanc from Napa Valley, which has layers of flavor that will stand up to this dish.

4 servings

PER SERVING: 795 calories, 44.5 g total fat (23 g saturated fat), 38 g protein, 62 g carbohydrate, 350 mg cholesterol, 880 mg sodium, 3.5 g fiber

Goat Cheesecake with Macadamia Nuts and Fresh Berries

Although most people would not be able to identify the goat cheese in this cheesecake, it's the ingredient that gives the dessert its divine flavor and silky texture. Macadamia nuts are a tasty, crunchy addition to the crust and top of the cheesecake. As with any cheesecake recipe, take care not to overmix this one. Overbeating the eggs will aerate the batter and cause the cake to fall in the center as it cools.

CRUST
1 cup shortbread cookie crumbs (about 7 cookies, crushed)
¾ cup macadamia nuts, toasted, ground*
2 tablespoons sugar
1 teaspoon cinnamon
¼ cup unsalted butter, melted

FILLING
8 oz. mild soft goat cheese, softened
3 (8-oz.) pkg. cream cheese, softened
1⅓ cups sugar
4 eggs
½ teaspoon salt
2 tablespoons nut liqueur (macadamia, Frangelico or amaretto) or orange juice
½ cup whole macadamia nuts, toasted*

SAUCE
4 cups strawberries, thinly sliced
¼ cup sugar
1 to 2 tablespoons nut liqueur, if desired

1 Place oven rack in lower third of oven. Heat oven to 350°F. In medium bowl, stir together all crust ingredients until crumbs hold together. Press into bottom of 9½-inch springform pan. Bake 8 to 10 minutes or until light golden brown. Cool on wire rack while making filling.

2 In large bowl, beat goat cheese and cream cheese at medium speed 1 minute or until smooth. Add 1⅓ cups sugar; beat at medium speed 30 seconds, scraping sides of bowl occasionally. At low speed, beat in eggs one at a time, mixing just until combined. Beat in salt and 2 tablespoons liqueur.

3 Wrap outside of springform pan with large piece of heavy-duty foil. Place in large shallow roasting or broiler pan. Pour filling into cooled crust. Sprinkle whole nuts over surface of cake. Add enough hot tap water to come halfway up sides of springform pan.

4 Bake 45 to 55 minutes or until edges are puffed and top looks dull and is dry to the touch. Center should move slightly when side

Goat Cheese with Macadamia Nuts and Fresh Berries

of pan is tapped. Cool completely on wire rack. Cover and refrigerate at least 4 hours or overnight, until cheesecake is thoroughly chilled.

5 Two hours before serving, in small bowl, stir together all sauce ingredients. Cover; let stand at room temperature until ready to serve. Serve sauce with cheesecake. Refrigerate leftovers.

TIP *To toast macadamia nuts, spread on baking sheet; bake at 375°F. for 10 minutes or until lightly browned. To grind, place in food processor; pulse until finely ground.

WINE It is important to pair this cheesecake with a delicate dessert wine to let the complex flavors of the dish emerge. Try the Beaulieu Vineyard Muscat from California or a slightly sweet, light-as-a-feather sparkling Moscato d'Asti from Saracco.

12 servings

PER SERVING: 610 calories, 43.5 g total fat (20.5 g saturated fat), 11.5 g protein, 47 g carbohydrate, 165 mg cholesterol, 420 mg sodium, 3 g fiber

Mediterranean Roast Chicken with Goat Cheese Stuffing

Mediterranean Roast Chicken with Goat Cheese Stuffing

This dish was inspired by flavors of the south of France. You'll love the cheesy stuffing, redolent of herbs and olives. If you can't find basil oil, we give a tip for making your own.

- 2 teaspoons olive oil
- 1 large shallot, finely chopped
- 1 large garlic clove, minced
- 6 oz. soft goat cheese with herbs
- ¼ cup (1 oz.) shredded aged goat cheese
- ¼ cup pitted kalamata olives, chopped
- 3 tablespoons chopped fresh basil
- ¼ teaspoon sea salt, divided
- ¼ teaspoon freshly ground pepper, divided
- 4 bone-in chicken breast halves with skin*
- 2 tablespoons basil-flavored olive oil**

1 Heat oven to 375°F. Heat 2 teaspoons oil in small skillet over medium heat until hot. Add shallot and garlic; cook 30 to 60 seconds or until fragrant. Place in medium bowl.
2 Add herbed cheese, aged cheese, olives, basil and ⅛ teaspoon each of the salt and pepper. Stir until blended.
3 Line shallow baking pan with foil. With fingertips, make pocket under chicken skin. Place stuffing in pocket; place chicken in pan. Brush chicken with basil-flavored oil; sprinkle with remaining ⅛ teaspoon each of the salt and pepper. Bake 35 to 40 minutes or until chicken is no longer pink in center and juices run clear, brushing with oil halfway through baking.

TIPS *Look for chicken breasts that do not have torn or incomplete skin because the skin helps keep the chicken moist.

**To make your own basil-flavored olive oil, place 2 tablespoons extra-virgin olive oil in small food processor. Add 1 tablespoon chopped fresh basil. Blend until smooth.

WINE This dish definitely needs a flavorful Chardonnay. One fine value is the R.H. Phillips from California. Château Ste. Michelle "Canoe Ridge" from Washington is richer yet not overpowering.

4 servings

PER SERVING: 440 calories, 31 g total fat (12 g saturated fat), 36.5 g protein, 3.5 g carbohydrate, 125 mg cholesterol, 410 mg sodium, .5 g fiber

Hallie Harron is the chef-owner of the French Culinary Cottage in Phoenix, Arizona.

Guide to Goat Cheese

Goat cheese is usually thought of as the fresh, white, creamy version often sold in logs. But goat's milk is made into several types of cheeses: fresh, ripened and aged. The cheese can vary in shape and taste, and its texture can range from soft to semi-soft to hard.

Fresh goat cheese is made from an acidic uncooked curd. This curd gives the cheese its characteristic light tangy taste. Very moist, soft fresh goat cheese is sold in containers and has the consistency of yogurt. It can be used in recipes that call for a very soft cheese, but it does not work well in recipes calling for crumbled cheese. Other fresh goat cheeses are drained and then placed in molds for shaping before being sold. They have a variety of textures, and shapes range from rounds and logs to pyramids and crottins (flat-topped pyramids). Fresh goat cheese also can be flavored with herbs or spices, coated in ash or wrapped in grape leaves. To preserve freshness, these types often are sold in vacuum-packed containers. Fresh goat cheese can be tossed with pasta, used in fillings or stuffings, sprinkled on pizza or salads, and used in baked desserts.

Ripened goat cheese is made from the same uncooked curd as fresh goat cheese, but after the cheese is drained and molded, it's placed in a special chamber to ripen for two to five weeks. During the ripening process, a mold begins to develop on the outside of the cheese. This mold is integral to the flavor and texture of the cheese. The flavor of ripened goat cheese is softer and sweeter than fresh goat cheese because the tangy zing of the uncooked curd mellows during the ripening process. Ripened goat cheese is used less frequently in cooking than fresh goat cheese because it doesn't melt or blend easily. Try it in gratins or recipes calling for a Brie- or Camembert-style cheese. It's also perfect served on its own or accompanying fresh figs or other fruit.

Aged goat cheese is also ripened, but for a much longer time. It differs from the other types because it's made with a cooked curd. There are many varieties of European aged goat cheeses but fewer American varieties — it's still a new process for U.S. cheesemakers. Aged goat cheese can range in texture from very firm grating cheese that is low in moisture to cheese that becomes softer and creamier as it ages. It has an outside rind that forms during the aging process after the mold dies. This rind can have many different textures, from soft to firm, depending on the style of cheese. Many aged goat cheeses can be used in cooking, especially those that can be grated. They have higher fat content than fresh or ripened cheese and, therefore, melt better.

—*Janice Cole*

Roasted Peaches with Gorgonzola, Toasted Almonds and Honey

Cheese of Course

Savor the flavors of cheese before, during or after a meal.

Text and Recipes by Janet Fletcher

If you've traveled to France, you've probably encountered the French custom of serving a cheese course at the end of the meal. Whether you're dining in a private home, a country bistro or the most elegant Parisian restaurant, a tantalizing platter of cheeses inevitably comes to the table, usually after the main course. Serving a cheese course allows you to slow down the pace of a meal, spend a little more time with friends and enjoy another glass of wine.

You can serve cheese French-style at the end of the meal, or welcome your guests American-style with a cheese course before dinner. You can offer a single cheese or a selection of several cheeses. Either way, pair cheese with creative accompaniments to heighten the flavors of the cheeses and the experience. The French typically serve cheese simply, with bread and fruit. Or try the food pairings suggested here, from Roasted Peaches with Gorgonzola to Baked Feta with Sweet and Hot Peppers.

With so many cheeses available at markets and specialty shops, the cheese course may become a standard part of your meals.

Roasted Peaches with Gorgonzola, Toasted Almonds and Honey

Italian Gorgonzola comes in two styles: dolce, a milder, younger style; and naturale, sometimes called mountain Gorgonzola, a more aged version with a stronger flavor. Either style works in this recipe.

- 2 large peaches or nectarines, halved
- 4 tablespoons honey, divided
- ½ lb. Italian Gorgonzola
- 2 tablespoons toasted slivered almonds*

1 Heat oven to 325°F. Place peach halves, cut side up, in 8-inch square baking pan. Fill each cavity with ½ tablespoon of the honey. Pour ⅓ cup water into pan. Bake, uncovered, 30 minutes or until peaches are tender, occasionally spooning pan juices over fruit.
2 Place peaches on plate to cool. Baking juices should be slightly thickened. If not, pour into small saucepan; boil over medium-high heat until syrupy. Spoon baking juices over peaches; let cool until barely warm. Remove peach skins; cut each

half into 4 wedges.
3 Divide cheese among 4 plates. Drizzle each with ½ tablespoon of the honey; sprinkle each with ½ tablespoon of the almonds. Arrange peach slices next to cheese.
TIP *To toast almonds, place on baking sheet; bake at 375°F. for 6 minutes or until golden brown.
WINE B&G Vouvray from France has citrus fruit and a slightly sweet character, which pairs well with this cheese dish. Saracco Moscato d'Asti from Italy also works; it's slightly sparkling with a hint of sweetness and is light as a feather.

4 servings

PER SERVING: 320 calories, 18.5 g total fat (11 g saturated fat), 13.5 g protein, 28.5 g carbohydrate, 45 mg cholesterol, 790 mg sodium, 2 g fiber

Whole Wheat Walnut Bread with Triple-Cream Cheese

Plan to start this bread at least one day ahead because the starter needs to sit from 12 to 24 hours before the dough is made. Triple-cream cheeses are extra rich and creamy because of their high butterfat content. Good choices are Explorateur, Brillat-Savarin, Pierre Robert and St. André.

STARTER
- ¼ cup warm water (105°F. to 115°F.)
- ½ teaspoon active dry yeast
- ½ cup lukewarm water (90°F. to 95°F.)
- 1 cup whole wheat flour

DOUGH
- ½ cup warm water (105°F. to 115°F.)
- 1¾ teaspoons active dry yeast
- 1 cup toasted walnuts, chopped*
- 1¼ teaspoons salt
- 2 to 2¼ cups all-purpose flour
- 1 tablespoon cornmeal
- 1 lb. triple-cream cheese

1 To make starter, place ¼ cup warm water in large bowl; sprinkle with ½ teaspoon yeast. Let stand 2 minutes to soften. Whisk with fork; let stand 10 minutes. Stir in lukewarm water and whole wheat flour until smooth. Cover with plastic wrap; let stand at room temperature at least 12 hours or up to 24 hours.
2 To make dough, place ½ cup warm water in large bowl; sprinkle with 1¾ teaspoons yeast. Let stand 2 minutes to soften. Whisk with fork; let stand 10 minutes. Stir in starter, walnuts and salt. Gradually mix in 1¾ to 2 cups of the all-purpose flour; turn out

onto lightly floured surface. Knead 8 to 10 minutes or until smooth and elastic, adding additional flour as necessary to keep dough from sticking.

3 Lightly oil another large bowl. Shape dough into ball; place in bowl. Turn to coat with oil. Cover tightly with plastic wrap; let rise in cool place (for a slow rise) 1 1/2 hours or until doubled. Gently punch dough to deflate; shape into 7-inch round. Lightly dust baking sheet with cornmeal; place dough on baking sheet. Cover; let rise in cool place 1 1/2 hours or until doubled.

4 Heat oven to 425°F. With sharp knife, make 3 slashes in top of bread. Bake 30 minutes. Reduce oven temperature to 325°F.; continue baking 15 to 20 minutes or until golden brown and loaf sounds hollow when tapped on bottom. Cool completely on wire rack. Serve with cheese.

TIP *To toast walnuts, spread on baking sheet; bake at 375°F. for 7 to 10 minutes or until lightly browned. Cool.

12 servings

PER Serving: 280 calories, 18.5 g total fat (9 g saturated fat), 7 g protein, 22.5 g carbohydrate, 40 mg cholesterol, 355 mg sodium, 2 g fiber

Selecting & Serving Cheese

To select and serve cheese at its best, enlist the help of a knowledgeable merchant. If possible, purchase cheese from a store that cuts and wraps cheese to order, so you can taste before you buy. Your familiarity with cheese will grow quickly if you always buy at least one cheese you've never tasted before. Follow these guidelines when assembling and serving a cheese platter.

- Aim for variety in texture, taste and appearance. Contrast a young California goat cheese with an aged Dutch Gouda; a silky triple-cream, such as Brillat-Savarin, with a firm Vermont cheddar; a mild Gruyère with a pungent Gorgonzola. To guarantee variety, choose a cow's milk, goat's milk and sheep's milk cheese. Selecting varied shapes — small disks, large rounds, pyramids and wedges — adds eye appeal.

- Limit the selection you serve to three or four cheeses. Palates become weary beyond that point, and guests may have trouble remembering what's what.

- Always serve cheese at room temperature for optimum flavor and texture. Although many experts recommend taking the cheese out of the refrigerator one hour ahead, you should allow more time for a large wedge.

- Remove any paper or foil wrap, but leave the rind in place. The cheese's rind is part of its natural beauty, and guests can cut it away or not. For a cheese platter passed at the table, don't portion the cheese for your guests; let them serve themselves as much as they like.

- For a serving platter, any attractive flat surface can be used: a wooden bread board, a ceramic platter, a slab of marble or granite, a wicker tray or even a cake stand. If you will be passing it at the table, make sure the tray is light enough to handle comfortably.

- If possible, place a serving tool with each cheese. Use a salad or butter knife with soft, creamy cheeses and a sharper knife with firm cheeses.

Sesame Breadsticks with Manchego and Green Olives

Sesame Breadsticks with Manchego and Green Olives

The breadsticks are at their best served warm from the oven. If you can't find manchego, substitute Tuscan pecorino or French P'tit Basque. Use any favorite green olive, seasoned or unseasoned.

DOUGH
- ¾ cup warm water (105°F. to 115°F.)
- 1½ teaspoons active dry yeast
- 1 tablespoon olive oil
- 1 teaspoon salt
- 1½ to 1¾ cups all-purpose flour
- ½ cup sesame seeds

CHEESE
- ½ lb. Spanish manchego or other aged sheep's milk cheese, cut into 16 thin slices
- 2 cups green olives

1 Place water in large bowl; sprinkle with yeast. Let stand 2 minutes to soften; whisk with fork to blend. Let stand 10 minutes. Stir in oil, salt and 1½ cups of the flour. (Dough will be very sticky.) Turn out onto lightly floured surface; sprinkle dough with flour. Knead 5 minutes or until smooth and elastic, adding additional flour as needed. Shape into ball. Lightly coat large bowl with oil. Place dough in bowl; turn to coat with oil. Cover with plastic wrap; let rise in cool place (for a slow rise) 1½ hours or until doubled.

2 Turn dough out onto surface lightly coated with olive oil (dough will be very sticky). With oiled fingertips, press dough into 12x7-inch rectangle. Sprinkle with ¼ cup of the sesame seeds; gently press seeds into dough. Turn; sprinkle with remaining ¼ cup sesame seeds. Press gently into dough. Cover with clean towel; let rise 1 hour or until puffy.

3 Meanwhile, place baking stone on bottom rack in oven. Heat oven to 425°F. Lightly brush 2 heavy baking sheets with olive oil.

4 Starting with short end, cut dough into ½-inch strips. Place strips on baking sheets, being careful not to stretch dough.

5 Bake 1 pan at a time, placing baking sheet on baking stone. Bake 14 to 16 minutes or until golden brown and crisp. Cool breadsticks briefly on wire rack. Serve warm with cheese and olives. (Breadsticks may be made up to 1 day ahead. To warm, place on baking sheet. Bake at 350°F. for 10 minutes or until warm.)

WINE This dish calls for some easy-to-drink reds. Try the lightly spicy Santa Sofia Valpolicella Classico from the Veneto region in northern Italy. Bolla Merlot "Colforte" is a well-made, flavorful Italian wine that also works well.

8 servings

PER SERVING: 285 calories, 18.5 g total fat (6.5 g saturated fat), 12 g protein, 19.5 g carbohydrate, 25 mg cholesterol, 1450 mg sodium, 2 g fiber

Farmstead Cheddar with Baby Greens, Pear and Fennel

A farmhouse or farmstead cheese is made with milk from the cheesemaker's own herd. Delicious farmstead cheddars include Montgomery's and Keen's from England and Shelburne Farms from Vermont.

VINAIGRETTE
- 1 large shallot, finely minced
- 1½ tablespoons Champagne vinegar or white wine vinegar
- 4½ tablespoons walnut oil
- ¼ teaspoon sea salt
- ¼ teaspoon freshly ground pepper

SALAD
- 8 oz. mixed baby greens (10 cups)
- ½ large fennel bulb, fronds removed and discarded, cut crosswise into paper-thin slices
- 1 small ripe but firm red Bartlett pear, halved, thinly sliced
- ½ cup pecans, toasted, coarsely chopped*
- ¾ lb. farmstead cheddar, cut into 6 pieces

1 In small bowl, combine shallot and vinegar; let stand 30 minutes. Whisk in oil, salt and pepper.

2 Place mixed greens, fennel, pear slices and pecans in large bowl; toss with vinaigrette. Divide among 6 plates; place cheese wedge in center of each salad.

TIP *To toast pecans, spread on baking sheet; bake at 375°F. for 7 to 10 minutes or until light golden brown.

6 servings

PER SERVING: 405 calories, 35.5 g total fat (13.5 g saturated fat), 16 g protein, 8 g carbohydrate, 60 mg cholesterol, 440 mg sodium, 2.5 g fiber

Pairing Cheese with Wine & Other Foods

Wine is the classic companion for most cheeses, but which wines are best? A medium-bodied, dry red, such as Zinfandel or Pinot Noir, flatters a wide variety of cheeses. If you're serving a single cheese, the following guidelines should produce a good marriage.

- Serve young, crisp wines, such as Sauvignon Blanc, with young cheeses, such as fresh goat cheese or feta.

- Serve older wines with more mature cheeses, such as aged Burgundy or Cabernet Sauvignon with a two-year-old cheddar.

- Serve a wine from the same region as the cheese, such as Sonoma County Zinfandel with Sonoma County's Vella Dry Jack.

- Serve a dessert wine with blue cheeses, such as Sauternes with Roquefort.

Accompany cheeses with a plain baguette or nut bread to allow the cheeses' flavor and texture to shine. Herb breads, sweet breads or flavored crackers detract from the cheese. Toasted nuts and seasonal fruits — apricots, peaches and figs in summer; apples, grapes and pears in fall and winter — always make appealing cheese companions.

Baked Feta with Sweet and Hot Peppers

Baked Feta with Sweet and Hot Peppers

Creamy baked feta is a favorite Greek meze, or appetizer, served with crusty bread and kalamata olives. Look for an imported Greek, French or Bulgarian feta without much liquid. Serve with a chilled dry white wine, such as Sauvignon Blanc or Pinot Grigio.

- 1 tablespoon extra-virgin olive oil
- 1 small red bell pepper, halved, cut into ¼-inch strips
- ¼ teaspoon salt
- 1 (½-lb.) piece feta cheese
- ¾ teaspoon dried oregano
- ¼ cup pickled green pepperoncini, sliced

1 Heat oven to 375°F. Heat oil in medium skillet over medium heat until hot. Add red bell pepper and salt; cook 5 to 7 minutes or until peppers are tender but not mushy, stirring occasionally.

2 Slice feta into ½-inch-thick slices. Arrange in one layer in shallow 9-inch oval or round baking dish; sprinkle with oregano. Top with red bell pepper and pepperoncini.

3 Bake 12 to 14 minutes or until cheese is soft and oil bubbles. Serve warm with crusty bread.

WINE Peter Zemmer Pinot Grigio from northern Italy is crisp and flavorful, while St. Supéry Sauvignon Blanc from Napa marries well with the peppers in this appetizer.

6 servings

PER SERVING: 125 calories, 10.5 g total fat (6 g saturated fat), 5.5 g protein, 2.5 g carbohydrate, 35 mg cholesterol, 530 mg sodium, .5 g fiber

Janet Fletcher is a food writer based in Napa Valley, California. She's the author of *The Cheese Course* (Chronicle Books).

Roasted Butternut Squash Salad

Cherry Tomato Pasta
with Goat Cheese

Shaved Fennel and
Pomegranate Salad

Carrot, Cumin and Coriander
Soup and Chive Rolls

Soups, Salads & Sides

Tortellini Salad with
Broccoli, Mushrooms
and Tomatoes

Wild Mushroom, Smoked Chicken and Corn Chowder served with Roasted Red Pepper-Cornmeal Scones

Heartland Soups & Breads

The nourishing foods of the Midwest inspire a trio of comforting soups & breads.

Text and Recipes by Judith Fertig

In Kansas, the heart of the Midwest, you never know what to expect at this time of year. As winter loosens its grip, the weather becomes uncertain. One day might be drenched in sun and warmth, while the next could bring ice and snow. While milder days are just ahead, you're still in battle mode against the elements. In this season of uncertainty, Midwesterners find comfort in food: a simple supper of homemade soup and bread to nourish both body and soul.

The Midwestern cook's repertoire is full of flavorful soups and breads, inspired by the region's rich store of ingredients. Hickory or apple-smoked beef, pork and chicken. Hearty Kansas City-style steak. Mellow corn from nearby fields. Healthy root vegetables. And wheat that's grown, harvested and milled on the prairie.

Quick preparation makes these dishes even more appealing. With the help of convenience foods, such as canned broth and self-rising flour, you can put these soups and breads on the table in less than an hour. A heartwarming meal that's easy on the cook — what could be better?

Wild Mushroom, Smoked Chicken and Corn Chowder

This soup gets its smoky flavor from dried wild mushrooms and smoked chicken. Pair it with Roasted Red Pepper-Cornmeal Scones.

- 6 strips thick-sliced bacon, diced
- 1 large onion, chopped
- 1 red bell pepper, chopped
- 1 green bell pepper, chopped
- 3 cups frozen shoepeg corn, thawed, divided
- 1½ cups (8 oz.) chopped smoked chicken or turkey
- 3 medium red potatoes, peeled, chopped
- ½ cup (½ oz.) sliced dried wild mushrooms
- ¾ teaspoon salt
- ¼ teaspoon cayenne pepper
- ⅛ teaspoon freshly ground black pepper
- 4 cups water
- 2 cups half-and-half, divided

1 In large pot or Dutch oven, cook bacon over medium-high heat 4 to 6 minutes or until browned. Place on paper-towel-lined plate.

2 Drain all but 1 tablespoon of the drippings from pot; cook onion, red bell pepper and green bell pepper 5 minutes or until crisp-tender. Return bacon to pot. Stir in 2 cups of the corn, chicken, potatoes, mushrooms, salt, cayenne pepper and black pepper. Add 4 cups water or enough to cover. Partially cover pot and bring to a boil. Reduce heat to low; cook 30 minutes.

3 Meanwhile, in blender or food processor, blend remaining 1 cup corn and 1 cup of the half-and-half until almost smooth. Just before serving, stir pureed corn mixture and remaining 1 cup half-and-half into soup. Bring just to a simmer. (Do not let boil; soup will curdle.)

6 (1⅓-cup) servings

PER SERVING: 335 calories, 16 g total fat (8 g saturated fat), 14.5 g protein, 36 g carbohydrate, 55 mg cholesterol, 895 mg sodium, 4 g fiber

Roasted Red Pepper-Cornmeal Scones

Roasted red peppers flavor a scone that is savory, delicious and easy to prepare. Serve the scones as part of a fireside meal with hearty, savory chowder.

- 2 cups all-purpose flour
- ½ cup cornmeal
- 2 teaspoons chopped fresh thyme or 1 teaspoon dried
- 2 teaspoons baking powder
- ¼ teaspoon cream of tartar
- ½ teaspoon salt
- 1 egg, beaten
- 1 teaspoon packed brown sugar
- ½ cup chopped roasted red bell pepper
- 1 cup buttermilk
- 1 egg white, beaten until frothy

1 Heat oven to 425°F. Grease baking sheet or line with parchment paper. In large bowl, stir together flour, cornmeal, thyme, baking powder, cream of tartar and salt.

2 In small bowl, beat together egg and brown sugar; stir in roasted bell pepper. Make well in center of flour mixture; add egg mixture and buttermilk. With fork, blend into flour mixture until soft dough forms. (If dough is too stiff, add additional buttermilk; if too sticky, add additional flour.)

3 Turn dough out onto floured surface; gently form into 8-inch round. Place on baking sheet. Lightly score top into 8 wedges; brush with egg white.

Kansas City Steak Soup and Golden Wheat and Cheddar Loaves

4 Bake at 425°F. for 5 minutes. Reduce temperature to 375°F.; bake an additional 30 to 35 minutes or until lightly browned and bottom sounds hollow when tapped. Cool 15 minutes on wire rack; for a softer crust, wrap warm loaf in towel. Serve warm.

8 scones

PER SCONE: 175 calories, 1.5 g total fat (.5 g saturated fat), 6 g protein, 33.5 g carbohydrate, 30 mg cholesterol, 310 mg sodium, 1.5 g fiber

Kansas City Steak Soup

Dry red wine and thyme add sophisticated flavor to this Kansas City steakhouse favorite. Serve it with warm Golden Wheat and Cheddar Loaves.

- 1 tablespoon olive oil
- 1 lb. New York strip or rib-eye steak, cut into ½-inch pieces
- ¼ teaspoon freshly ground pepper
- 3 tablespoons butter
- ½ cup chopped celery
- ½ cup chopped carrots
- ½ cup chopped onions
- ¼ cup all-purpose flour
- 1 (14.5-oz.) can diced tomatoes, undrained
- 3 (14-oz.) cans beef broth
- ½ cup dry red wine
- ½ teaspoon dried thyme

1 Heat oil in large pot or nonreactive Dutch oven over medium-high heat until hot. Add beef; sprinkle with pepper. Cook 1 minute or just until edges begin to brown. Remove from pot; place on plate.

2 In same large pot, melt butter over medium heat. Add celery, carrots and onions; cook 2 minutes. Add flour; cook 3 minutes, stirring to scrape up brown bits from bottom of pot. Stir in tomatoes, broth, wine and thyme. Bring to a boil. Reduce heat to medium; simmer 12 to 15 minutes or until vegetables are tender.

3 Stir beef and drippings into soup. Cook 2 minutes for medium-rare or until of desired doneness.

(about 1¾-cup) servings

PER SERVING: 365 calories, 19.5 g total fat (8.5 g saturated fat), 30 g protein, 17 g carbohydrate, 80 mg cholesterol, 1615 mg sodium, 2.5 g fiber

Golden Wheat and Cheddar Loaves

These chewy, crusty loaves bring the bounty of prairie wheat fields to your dinner table. They've got all the aroma of a traditional yeast bread, but they don't take all the time. Quick-rise yeast shortens proofing time, and smaller pans trim baking time.

- 2 cups whole wheat flour
- 1¾ cups all-purpose flour
- 1 (¼-oz.) pkg. quick-rise yeast
- 1¼ teaspoons salt
- 1½ cups (6 oz.) shredded sharp cheddar cheese, divided
- 1¾ cups very warm (120°F. to 130°F.) water
- 2 tablespoons vegetable oil

1 Heat oven to 350°F. Spray 2 (7x4x2-inch) loaf pans* with nonstick cooking spray.

2 In large bowl, stir together whole wheat flour, all-purpose flour, yeast, salt and 1 cup of the cheese. Make well in center of flour mixture; add water and oil. Gradually stir dry ingredients into water mixture until soft dough forms. If dough is too sticky, add additional flour 1 tablespoon at a time.

3 Turn out dough onto lightly floured surface; divide in half. Shape into loaves; place in pans. Cover with towel; let stand 30 minutes or until slightly risen. Sprinkle top of each loaf with ¼ cup of the remaining cheese.

4 Bake 30 to 35 minutes or until browned and loaves sound hollow when tapped or internal temperature reaches 190°F. Cool on wire rack.

TIP *Two (8x4x2-inch) loaf pans may be used, but the loaves will not rise as high.

2 (14-slice) loaves

PER SLICE: 80 calories, 2.5 g total fat (1.5 g saturated fat), 3.5 g protein, 12 g carbohydrate, 5 mg cholesterol, 140 mg sodium, 1.5 g fiber

Carrot, Cumin and Coriander Soup

During prairie winters, root vegetables sustained farm families. Today, they show up in soups like this one that's not only tasty but also low-fat. Pair the soup with Chive Rolls.

SOUP
- 4 cups chopped carrots (8 medium)
- 1 cup peeled chopped russet potato (about 1 medium)
- ¾ cup chopped onions
- 1 (49-oz.) can reduced-sodium chicken broth (5¾ cups)
- 2 teaspoons ground coriander
- 1 teaspoon ground cumin
- ½ teaspoon salt
- ¼ teaspoon freshly ground pepper

GARNISH
- ¼ cup plain yogurt
- 2 tablespoons coarsely chopped fresh cilantro

1 In large saucepan, combine all soup ingredients; bring to a boil over medium-high heat. Reduce heat to low; simmer 25 to 30 minutes or until potatoes are fork-tender.

2 Place mixture in large bowl. Puree in batches in blender or food

Carrot, Cumin and Coriander Soup and Chive Rolls

processor. (Be careful when pureeing hot liquids.) Return to saucepan.

3 Heat over medium heat until hot. Garnish each serving with dollop of yogurt; sprinkle with cilantro.

4 servings

PER SERVING: 170 calories, 3 g total fat (1 g saturated fat), 10 g protein, 27 g carbohydrate, 0 mg cholesterol, 1015 mg sodium, 5.5 g fiber

Chive Rolls

These quick rolls can be made while the soup is simmering.

- 1 cup self-rising flour*
- ¾ cup milk
- 3 tablespoons mayonnaise
- 2 tablespoons chopped fresh chives
- ¼ teaspoon white pepper

1 Heat oven to 350°F. Spray 6 muffin cups with nonstick cooking spray. In medium bowl, whisk together all ingredients just until moistened. Spoon dough into muffin cups, filling two-thirds full.

2 Bake 20 to 25 minutes or until lightly browned and toothpick inserted in center comes out clean. Serve warm.

TIP *To substitute for self-rising flour, use 1 cup all-purpose flour, 1½ teaspoons baking powder and ⅛ teaspoon salt.

6 rolls

PER ROLL: 135 calories, 6.5 g total fat (1 g saturated fat), 3 g protein, 17 g carbohydrate, 5 mg cholesterol, 320 mg sodium, .5 g fiber

Judith Fertig is a Kansas City-based food writer. She is the author of *Prairie Home Breads* (Harvard Common Press).

Bacon-Tomato Salad

Simply Tomatoes

Summer tomatoes shine in these easily prepared dishes.

Text and Recipes by Georgeanne Brennan

Nothing is more symbolic of late summer than fresh, ripe tomatoes. By mid-August, gardens and markets are overflowing with this luscious fruit in an amazing array of colors, shapes and sizes, and we're searching for easy ways to use them.

Many cooks delight in a simple platter of four or five different kinds of tomatoes, sliced and splashed with olive oil and a little chopped basil; or they chop them up with chiles and cilantro to make a salsa medley. Tomatoes also can be roasted, grilled, fried, broiled or sautéed and added to pot roasts or chicken, cooked into sauces or soups, or used in omelets, salads, sandwiches or stews. If you're afraid you won't get your fill this season, fry tomatoes for breakfast, grill them for lunch and then roast them for dinner.

August is the perfect month for tomato lovers. With the number of varieties and limitless ways to use them, you'll never go wanting.

Bacon-Tomato Salad

This main dish salad, a variation on a bacon, lettuce and tomato sandwich, highlights the juicy richness of beefsteak tomatoes. Beefsteaks, the ultimate slicing tomatoes, are prized for salads and sandwiches because they are plump, meaty and have few seeds.

- 12 slices bacon
- 3 tablespoons extra-virgin olive oil, divided
- 3 thin slices baguette or other rustic bread
- 3 tablespoons mayonnaise
- 1 teaspoon freshly ground pepper, divided
- 5 cups romaine lettuce, torn into bite-size pieces
- 4 beefsteak tomatoes or 6 medium tomatoes, sliced ½ inch thick
- ¼ cup coarsely chopped fresh basil

1 Heat oven to 375°F. Place bacon on rimmed baking sheet; bake 25 to 30 minutes or until crisp. Place on paper towels to drain. When cool, coarsely crumble.
2 Heat 2 tablespoons of the oil in small skillet over medium-high heat until hot. Add bread slices; fry 3 to 4 minutes or until light golden brown, turning once. Place on paper towels to drain. When cool, break each slice into 4 or 5 pieces.
3 In large bowl, stir together remaining 1 tablespoon oil, mayonnaise and ½ teaspoon of the pepper. Add lettuce; toss to coat. Arrange lettuce on serving platter. Scatter bread over lettuce. Top with tomato; sprinkle with remaining ½ teaspoon pepper and crumbled bacon. Garnish with basil.
BEER/WINE There's no need for too-complicated or too-intense flavors here. Grolsch beer from Holland pairs nicely. If you prefer wine, try Louis Jadot Mâcon-Villages, a 100-percent Chardonnay from France.
4 servings

PER SERVING: 345 calories, 28.5 g total fat (6 g saturated fat), 9 g protein, 15 g carbohydrate, 25 mg cholesterol, 435 mg sodium, 3.5 g fiber

Grilled Tomato and Salmon Salad

This elegant salad works perfectly as a brunch or lunch dish. If you'd prefer to serve it as a first course, use only one salmon fillet.

VINAIGRETTE
- 3 tablespoons extra-virgin olive oil
- 2 tablespoons lemon juice
- 1 tablespoon grated lemon peel
- ½ teaspoon freshly ground pepper
- ¼ teaspoon salt

SALAD
- 2 (4-oz.) salmon fillets
- 2 medium tomatoes, sliced ½ inch thick
- ½ teaspoon freshly ground pepper
- ¼ teaspoon salt
- 2 cups mixed salad greens
- 2 tablespoons pine nuts, toasted*

1 In small bowl, whisk together all vinaigrette ingredients until blended; reserve 2 tablespoons of the vinaigrette.
2 Heat grill. Brush both sides of salmon and tomato slices with reserved 2 tablespoons of the vinaigrette. Sprinkle salmon with ½ teaspoon pepper and ¼ teaspoon salt. Place on gas grill over medium heat or on charcoal grill 4 to 6 inches from medium coals. Grill 5 to 7 minutes or until fish just begins to flake, turning once. During last 2 minutes of grilling time, place tomatoes on grill; grill 2 minutes or until tomatoes are slightly softened. *(Continued on page 33.)*

(Continued on page 33.)

Cherry Tomato Pasta
with Goat Cheese

3 Meanwhile, place greens in large bowl; toss with enough of the remaining vinaigrette to lightly coat greens. Place on serving plates; top with tomatoes. Place salmon on tomatoes; sprinkle with pine nuts. Drizzle with remaining vinaigrette.
TIP *Place nuts in dry skillet. Cook over medium heat 2 to 3 minutes or until nuts are light brown, stirring constantly.
WINE Rosemount Estate "Diamond Label" Chardonnay from Australia goes well with the salmon in this salad, as does Rodney Strong "Chalk Hill" Chardonnay from Sonoma.

2 servings

PER SERVING: 425 calories, 32 g total fat (5.5 g saturated fat), 27 g protein, 10.5 g carbohydrate, 75 mg cholesterol, 675 mg sodium, 3.5 g fiber

Cherry Tomato Pasta with Goat Cheese

In this easy summer dish, only the pasta is cooked.

- 8 oz. fettuccine
- 2 cups cherry tomatoes (mixed colors if possible), halved
- ½ cup lightly packed chopped fresh basil
- ½ teaspoon salt
- ½ teaspoon freshly ground pepper
- 2 tablespoons extra-virgin olive oil
- 3 tablespoons (1½ oz.) crumbled soft goat cheese

1 Cook fettuccine in large pot of boiling salted water 8 to 10 minutes or until al dente; drain.
2 Meanwhile, in large bowl, toss together tomatoes, basil, salt, pepper and oil. Stir in cheese. Immediately toss hot fettuccine with tomato mixture until cheese is melted.
WINE This dish calls for a richly flavored, slightly earthy white wine. E. Guigal Côtes du Rhône Blanc from France is a good choice. Or try Frog's Leap Sauvignon Blanc from Napa.

4 (1½-cup) servings

PER SERVING: 305 calories, 11.5 g total fat (3 g saturated fat), 9.5 g protein, 41.5 g carbohydrate, 60 mg cholesterol, 580 mg sodium, 3 g fiber

Balsamic-Marinated Tomato Sandwiches

Balsamic vinegar brings out the sweetness of tomatoes in this sandwich. Any leftover marinade can be used as a vinaigrette for a mixed green salad.

- ¼ cup extra-virgin olive oil
- 1 tablespoon balsamic vinegar
- 2 teaspoons red wine vinegar
- 1 tablespoon chopped fresh tarragon
- ½ teaspoon salt, divided
- ½ teaspoon freshly ground pepper, divided
- 1 garlic clove, minced
- 4 beefsteak tomatoes or 6 medium tomatoes, sliced ¼ inch thick
- 1 small red onion, thinly sliced
- 6 individual French bread loaves, split
- 6 leaves Boston lettuce or 1 cup arugula or watercress
- 2 avocados, sliced

1 In small bowl, whisk together oil, balsamic vinegar, red wine vinegar, tarragon, ¼ teaspoon each of the salt and pepper, and garlic. Place half of the tomato slices and half of the onion slices on platter or in shallow baking dish; drizzle with half of the olive oil mixture. Add remaining tomato and onion; drizzle with remaining olive oil mixture. Let stand at least 2 hours, spooning juices over tomato and onion 4 or 5 times.
2 To assemble sandwiches, place bread loaves, cut side up, on plates or serving platter; brush cut sides with marinade. Divide tomato and onion mixture among loaves. Top with lettuce and avocado; sprinkle with remaining ¼ teaspoon salt and pepper.

6 sandwiches

PER SANDWICH: 320 calories, 16 g total fat (2.5 g saturated fat), 7.5 g protein, 40 g carbohydrate, 0 mg cholesterol, 495 mg sodium, 7 g fiber

Roasted Tomato Soup

Roasted Tomato Soup

When choosing tomatoes for this soup, look for the sweetest and ripest ones you can find. Although any color can be used, try yellow tomatoes and a purple basil garnish for a spectacular presentation.

2 tablespoons olive oil
1 large garlic clove, minced
2 teaspoons minced fresh thyme
1 teaspoon salt
½ teaspoon freshly ground pepper
4 lb. tomatoes (about 10 medium)

2½ cups reduced-sodium chicken broth
3 tablespoons crème fraîche or sour cream, if desired*
3 tablespoons minced fresh basil

1 Heat oven to 400°F. In small bowl, stir together oil, garlic, thyme, salt and pepper. Remove core from tomatoes; brush whole tomatoes with oil mixture. Place in shallow baking pan.

2 Bake 35 to 45 minutes or until skins have split and tomatoes have slightly collapsed. Let cool 20 minutes or until tomatoes can be handled. Brush seasoning mixture off tomatoes; reserve. Remove and discard skins.

3 Put tomatoes, accumulated juices and seasoning mixture in large saucepan or nonreactive Dutch oven; bring to a boil over high heat. Reduce heat to medium-high to medium; boil 10 to 15 minutes or until slightly thickened, using spoon to stir and crush tomatoes. Add broth; bring to a boil. Reduce heat to medium to medium-low; simmer 15 minutes, stirring occasionally. If desired, puree slightly in blender or pass through food mill to remove seeds.

4 Pour into soup bowls. If desired, top each serving with crème fraîche; sprinkle with basil.

TIP *Crème fraîche is a slightly tangy, thickened cream. It can be found in the dairy section of gourmet supermarkets.

4 (1⅔-cup) servings

PER SERVING: 195 calories, 11 g total fat (2.5 g saturated fat), 7 g protein, 20.5 g carbohydrate, 5 mg cholesterol, 925 mg sodium, 4 g fiber

Georgeanne Brennan is a food writer in northern California. She spends part of the year in France, where she owns a cooking school.

Using Tomatoes

Tomatoes lend themselves to a variety of cooking methods. Each method gives the tomatoes different flavors, from smokiness after grilling to a caramelized taste when sautéed.

Roasting gives tomatoes an extra flavor dimension with very little effort. To roast tomatoes, cook them at 500°F. for 10 to 15 minutes or until the skins are plumped and just begin to split. Roasted tomatoes, seasoned with olive oil and herbs, can be made into sauces or soups. You also can dice them and toss them with corn to create a summer salsa or puree them with black olives to make a sauce for grilled steak or polenta.

Grilling tomatoes imbues them with a slightly smoky quality and starts to caramelize them. To grill sliced tomatoes, oil the grill or grilling pan thoroughly. If desired, season the tomatoes. Then cook the slices 2 to 4 minutes, turning once, or just until the slices are heated through. Serve grilled tomatoes with bacon and eggs for breakfast; add them to hamburgers or other hot sandwiches, such as roast pork or barbecued beef; or serve them on top of a green salad.

Broiling halved tomatoes is a classic French and English technique. In Provence, broiled tomatoes are liberally seasoned with minced garlic, parsley, salt, pepper and olive oil. In England, they usually are brushed with butter and sprinkled with parsley. To broil tomatoes, season them and place them 4 to 6 inches from the broiler for 2 to 5 minutes. Broiled tomatoes can be served as a first course or as an accompaniment to any dish; they are especially good with leg of lamb or roast beef.

Frying brings to mind green tomatoes cooked in seasoned flour and cornmeal or bread crumbs, but any firm, slightly underripe tomato can be given the same treatment. To fry tomatoes, slice them and pat them dry. In a shallow bowl, combine a little flour with salt and pepper. In another bowl, whisk together one egg and a bit of water. In another shallow bowl, stir together cornmeal or bread crumbs, salt, pepper and any other desired seasonings, such as grated Parmesan cheese, paprika or thyme. First dredge the tomato slices in the flour mixture. Then dip them in the egg mixture and dredge them in the cornmeal mixture. In a large skillet, heat some olive oil until almost smoking, then fry the tomatoes 4 to 8 minutes, turning once. Drain them on paper towels. Fried tomatoes can be served with garlic mayonnaise and fresh lemon wedges as a first course, or along with bacon or ham. They also can be served as a side dish.

Sautéing tomatoes until they are nearly caramelized brings out their sweetness. It's a quick and easy way to prepare a side dish or sauce. For a side dish, slice or chop the tomatoes and season them with fresh herbs. Add chopped sweet pepper and onion or zucchini; cook the mixture in olive oil 10 minutes or just until the tomatoes are barely soft but still hold their shape. For a sauce, cook the mixture 20 to 30 minutes or until it is thickened.

Fall Crudités Salad

Harvest Starters

Seasonal produce stars in full-flavored fall salads.

Text and Recipes by Mary Evans

Let's face it — it takes something special to make a salad shine. A mixture of greens and tomatoes is forgotten as quickly as it is prepared. For memorable salads, inspiration lies in seasonal produce prepared in fresh ways.

These recipes create handsomely rustic, full-flavored salads. Shaved fennel gives visual appeal to a salad studded with pomegranates and almonds. Matchstick-shaped ruby-red beets, pale celery root and green cabbage provide a striking presentation. Deep-orange butternut squash contrasts with soft greens and blue-veined Gorgonzola cheese.

With starters this good, the first course may become the one and only.

Fall Crudités Salad

Celery root, sometimes called celeriac, adds a mild celery flavor to salads. To use it, simply peel off its knobby brown exterior. Make sure to toss it with the vinaigrette right away to prevent it from darkening.

SALAD
- 3 medium to large beets*
- 2 cups julienned celery root
- 2 cups shredded cabbage
- 4 thin slices French bread, toasted
- 1 (3.5- to 4-oz.) log mild goat cheese, cut into 4 pieces

VINAIGRETTE
- 1½ tablespoons Dijon mustard
- 1 tablespoon white wine vinegar
- 1½ teaspoons mayonnaise
- ¼ teaspoon salt
- ⅛ teaspoon freshly ground pepper
- ¼ cup vegetable oil

1 Place beets in medium saucepan; add enough water to cover beets. Bring to a boil over high heat; boil 20 to 25 minutes or until tender. Drain; rinse under cold running water. When cool enough to handle, peel and julienne.
2 Meanwhile, in small bowl, whisk together mustard, vinegar,

mayonnaise, salt and pepper. Slowly whisk in oil until blended. Refrigerate until ready to use.
3 In small bowl, toss beets with 3 tablespoons of the vinaigrette. In second small bowl, toss celery root with 3 tablespoons of the vinaigrette. In third small bowl, toss cabbage with remaining vinaigrette. Arrange beets, celery root and cabbage on 4 salad plates.
4 Place toasted bread on microwave-safe plate; top each piece with piece of cheese. Microwave on high 15 seconds or until goat cheese is slightly warm. Place 1 bread slice in center of each salad. Serve immediately.
TIP *Canned beets can be substituted. Don't cook them; just drain and julienne.
4 servings

PER SERVING: 295 calories, 21 g total fat (6 g saturated fat), 6.5 g protein, 21.5 g carbohydrate, 25 mg cholesterol, 425 mg sodium, 4 g fiber

Winter Salad with Endive and Celery Root

Belgian endive and celery root are both popular ingredients in Parisian salads.

VINAIGRETTE
- 2 tablespoons Dijon mustard
- 3 tablespoons white wine vinegar
- ⅔ cup vegetable oil
- ¼ teaspoon salt
- ⅛ teaspoon freshly ground pepper

SALAD
- 4 cups mixed leaf lettuce
- 1 head Belgian endive, cut into ½-inch slices
- 1 cup diced celery root

1 In small bowl, whisk together mustard and vinegar. Slowly whisk in oil; season with salt and pepper.
2 In large bowl, combine lettuce, endive and celery root. Toss with vinaigrette until coated.
4 servings.

PER SERVING: 360 calories, 37 g total fat (5.5 g saturated fat), 0 mg cholesterol, 280 mg sodium, 5 g fiber

Shaved Fennel and Pomegranate Salad

Shaved Fennel and Pomegranate Salad

With their cheery color and sweet-tart flavor, pomegranates add a festive note to any dish. Remove the seeds over a tray or bowl to keep the juice from staining countertops.

VINAIGRETTE
   1 tablespoon raspberry vinegar
   ½ teaspoon Dijon mustard
   1½ teaspoons chopped fresh
        tarragon
   ⅛ teaspoon salt
   ⅛ teaspoon freshly ground pepper

   3 tablespoons mild extra-
        virgin olive oil
SALAD
   6 cups torn leaf lettuce
   1⅓ cups shaved or thinly sliced
        fennel*
        Seeds from 1 pomegranate
        (about 1½ cups)
   ¼ cup toasted sliced almonds**

1 In small bowl, whisk together vinegar, mustard, tarragon, salt and pepper. Slowly whisk in oil until blended.

2 When ready to serve, in large bowl, toss lettuce with vinaigrette. Divide lettuce among 4 salad plates. Sprinkle with fennel, pomegranate seeds and almonds. Serve immediately.

TIPS *To shave fennel, cut fennel bulb in half. Slice into paper-thin slices using mandoline or vegetable slicer. Place in ice water 20 to 60 minutes or until crisp.

**To toast almonds, place on baking sheet; bake at 375°F. for 5 minutes or until golden brown.

6 (1⅓-cup) servings

PER SERVING: 110 calories, 9 g total fat (1 g saturated fat), 2 g protein, 7.5 g carbohydrate, 0 mg cholesterol, 65 mg sodium, 2.5 g fiber

Roasted Butternut Squash Salad

Roasted Butternut Squash Salad

If there's any squash left over, roast and mash it and use it in soups or muffins. Serve this robust salad as a first course or as a side dish to roast pork or chicken.

SALAD
- 3 cups thickly sliced (½ inch) peeled halved butternut squash
- 1 tablespoon plus 2 teaspoons vegetable oil, divided
- ¼ cup packed brown sugar
- 2 teaspoons water
- ¼ teaspoon freshly ground pepper
- ½ cup walnut halves
- 6 cups torn romaine lettuce
- 1 cup (4 oz.) crumbled Gorgonzola cheese

VINAIGRETTE
- 1 tablespoon port or cranberry juice
- 1 teaspoon balsamic vinegar
- ½ teaspoon Dijon mustard
- ¼ teaspoon dried thyme
- ⅛ teaspoon salt
- ⅛ teaspoon freshly ground pepper
- 1 tablespoon minced shallots
- 2 tablespoons walnut or olive oil

1 Heat oven to 400°F. In shallow 15x10-inch baking pan, toss squash with 2 teaspoons of the vegetable oil. Bake 45 minutes or until golden brown, turning halfway through.
2 In small bowl, whisk together port, balsamic vinegar, mustard, thyme, salt and ⅛ teaspoon pepper; whisk in shallots. Slowly whisk in walnut oil until blended.

3 In medium skillet, stir together remaining 1 tablespoon vegetable oil, brown sugar, water and ¼ teaspoon pepper. Cook over medium heat, without stirring, until mixture is bubbling. Stir in nuts; cook an additional 30 seconds or until nuts are light brown. Turn out onto parchment paper; separate nuts with fork. When cool, break apart.

4 When squash is roasted, in large bowl, toss lettuce with vinaigrette. Place lettuce on serving platter. Top with squash; sprinkle with cheese and candied walnuts. Serve immediately.

6 (1⅓-cup) servings

PER SERVING: 280 calories, 19.5 g total fat (5 g saturated fat), 6.5 g protein, 22.5 g carbohydrate, 20 mg cholesterol, 330 mg sodium, 3.5 g fiber

Pear, Parsnip and Leek Salad

Parsnips come into their true glory after a hard frost, which brings out their sweet flavor. Look for parsnips that are firm, and peel them like a carrot to remove any wax.

SALAD
- 4 thick slices bacon
- 2 medium leeks, white part only, halved, cut into 1-inch pieces
- 3 small parsnips, quartered, cut into ¾-inch pieces
- 6 cups mixed salad greens
- 2 red Bartlett pears, unpeeled, cut into 8 wedges

VINAIGRETTE
- 1 tablespoon cider vinegar
- 1 teaspoon Dijon mustard
- 2 juniper berries, crushed, chopped*
- ⅛ teaspoon salt
- ⅛ teaspoon freshly ground pepper
- 3 tablespoons vegetable oil

1 Heat oven to 400°F. Cook bacon in large skillet over medium-low heat 12 minutes or until crisp; drain on paper towels. Remove skillet from heat; add leeks and parsnips. Toss with bacon drippings to coat. Spoon leeks and parsnips into shallow 15x10-inch baking pan. Bake 30 minutes or until tender and leeks are well browned.

2 Meanwhile, in small bowl, whisk together vinegar, mustard, juniper berries, salt and pepper. Slowly whisk in oil until blended.

3 When vegetables are cooked, in large bowl, toss greens with vinaigrette. Arrange greens on large platter or 4 individual salad plates. Top with roasted vegetables; crumble bacon over vegetables. Top with pear wedges.

TIP *Juniper berries, sold dried in the spice section, can be crushed by pressing them firmly with the side of a chef's knife.

6 (1⅓-cup) servings

PER SERVING: 200 calories, 14.5 g total fat (3.5 g saturated fat), 4.5 g protein, 15.5 g carbohydrate, 10 mg cholesterol, 215 mg sodium, 4 g fiber

Mary Evans is a Minneapolis-based food writer and cooking class instructor.

Steps to the Perfect Vinaigrette

Vinaigrettes are meant to enhance, not mask, the other ingredients in a salad. Use these tips to create vinaigrettes that make standout salads.

- Vinaigrettes should not be too acidic. A good rule is to use one part vinegar to three parts oil; sweeter vinegars can be used in higher concentrations. Use wine-, fruit- or rice-based vinegars for a tasty combination, but don't use plain white vinegar because its flavor is too harsh.

- If using Dijon mustard, whisk it into the vinegar before adding the oil. This helps keep everything in suspension and ensures that each salad element has just the right amount of vinegar and oil. The mustard also adds a nice zip to the finished vinaigrette.

- Add salt before adding oil because it dissolves better. Before tossing the salad, check the seasonings by dipping a lettuce leaf into the vinaigrette and tasting it. If the vinaigrette isn't flavorful enough, add more seasonings; if it's too strong, add more oil.

- All ingredients should be as dry as possible before being tossed with the vinaigrette. Otherwise, any clinging droplets of water will prevent the vinaigrette from sticking to the salad, instead causing it to pool at the bottom of the bowl.

Once you've mastered the basic vinaigrette, the fun begins. Experiment with the myriad flavored vinegars and oils on the market to invent your own combinations. Certain herbs complement greens and vegetables particularly well. Start by adding dill, tarragon and/or chives to create a classic vinaigrette. From there, branch out to basil, mint or exotic herbs, such as lovage, which has a pronounced celery flavor. Rich blue or hard cheeses, such as Parmesan, Romano or Asiago, make excellent additions.

Pear, Parsnip and Leek Salad

Roasted Ratatouille Salad

Picnic Pleasers

These salads are easy to make, easy to carry and easy to like.

Recipes by Beatrice Ojakangas

As the picnic season hits full stride, salads to go are in high demand. But after a few outings, the tried-and-true start to look tired, and the hunt begins for salads that are fresh and new.

Naturally, there are certain restrictions. Salads suitable for picnics have to be made ahead, and they must be easily transported. They also must be at their best when they sit for a bit and are eaten at room temperature.

These salads fit the picnic criteria. And you'll find a host of fresh flavors, from roasted vegetables in a rustic vinaigrette to sweet potatoes in a ginger-infused dressing. Enjoy the variety — there are enough choices to keep you happy for several picnics.

Roasted Ratatouille Salad

Roasting intensifies the flavors of the vegetables in this robust salad. Add a loaf of crispy French bread, some good cheese and chilled white wine to make a tasty meal.

- 1 small eggplant, cut into 1-inch cubes
- 1 medium zucchini, cut diagonally into ½-inch slices
- 1 medium yellow summer squash, cut diagonally into ½-inch slices
- 1 medium red or green bell pepper, cut lengthwise into ¾-inch pieces
- ½ large sweet onion, cut into 8 pieces
- 4 tablespoons olive oil, divided
- 1 teaspoon kosher (coarse) salt, divided
- 8 small red potatoes (about 1 lb.), unpeeled, quartered
- ½ garlic bulb (halved crosswise)
- 2 tablespoons balsamic vinegar
- 2 tablespoons chopped fresh basil

1 Arrange oven racks in upper and lower thirds of oven. Heat oven to 450°F. Line 2 large rimmed baking sheets with foil; spray with nonstick cooking spray.

2 In large bowl, combine eggplant, zucchini, squash, bell pepper and onion. Drizzle with 2 tablespoons of the oil; toss with ½ teaspoon of the salt. Spread vegetables in even layer on 1 baking sheet.

3 In same large bowl, toss potatoes with 1 tablespoon of the oil and remaining ½ teaspoon salt; spread in an even layer on second baking sheet. Brush cut edges of garlic with oil; place, cut side down, on second baking sheet. Bake vegetables and potatoes 15 to 20 minutes or until vegetables are crisp-tender and potatoes and garlic are tender, changing baking sheet positions halfway through baking. Cool to room temperature. Arrange cooked vegetables on serving platter.

4 Squeeze garlic cloves onto cutting board; mash with back of knife. In small bowl, whisk together mashed garlic, remaining 1 tablespoon oil and vinegar. Drizzle vegetables with vinaigrette; sprinkle with basil.

14 (½-cup) servings

PER SERVING: 80 calories, 4 g total fat (.5 g saturated fat), 1.5 g protein, 10.5 g carbohydrate, 0 mg cholesterol, 115 mg sodium, 2 g fiber

Lentil Salad with Olives and Sun-Dried Tomatoes

Lentils are legumes, as are dried beans, but they cook much faster, making them an ideal choice for summer salads. Look for green lentils in specialty food stores and red lentils (which turn yellow when cooked) in natural food stores or Middle Eastern or Indian markets.

- 1 cup green lentils
- 2½ cups water
- ½ cup red lentils
- 2 tablespoons olive oil
- ½ cup thinly sliced green onions
- ⅓ cup chopped drained oil-packed sun-dried tomatoes
- ⅓ cup pitted halved kalamata olives
- 2 tablespoons fresh lemon juice
- ½ teaspoon grated lemon peel
- ½ teaspoon kosher (coarse) salt
- ¼ teaspoon freshly ground pepper

1 In large saucepan, combine green lentils and water; bring to a boil. Reduce heat to low; cover and cook 10 minutes. Add red lentils; cook an additional 6 minutes or until lentils are tender but not mushy. Remove from heat; drain. Rinse under cold running water to cool. Place in large bowl; stir in oil.

2 Stir in all remaining ingredients. Cover; let stand at least 30 minutes. (Salad can be made up to 4 hours ahead. Cover and refrigerate. Bring to room temperature before serving.)

8 (½-cup) servings

PER SERVING: 170 calories, 5 g total fat (.5 g saturated fat), 10 g protein, 23 g carbohydrate, 0 mg cholesterol, 175 mg sodium, 10 g fiber

Couscous with Marinated Artichoke Hearts

Couscous with Marinated Artichoke Hearts

Inspired by the classic tabbouleh, this salad gets its terrific flavor from dill, parsley and a generous dose of lemon. Serve it alongside grilled chicken or tuna steaks.

1¾ cups couscous
2 cups boiling water
½ cup olive oil
1 teaspoon salt
¼ teaspoon freshly ground pepper
2 cups coarsely chopped marinated artichoke hearts
½ cup minced green onions
½ cup chopped fresh Italian parsley
1 tablespoon chopped fresh dill
3 tablespoons lemon juice
1 garlic clove, minced
½ cup toasted chopped walnuts*
1 cup (4 oz.) crumbled feta cheese

1 Place couscous in large bowl; cover with 2 cups boiling water. Stir; let stand 10 minutes or until water is absorbed. Stir in oil, salt and pepper.
2 Stir in artichoke hearts, green onions, parsley, dill, lemon juice and garlic. Transfer to serving bowl. Cover; let stand at least 30 minutes. (Salad can be made to this point up to 4 hours ahead. Cover and refrigerate. Bring to room temperature before serving.) Just before serving, sprinkle with walnuts and cheese.

TIP *To toast walnuts, spread on baking sheet; bake at 375°F. for 7 to 10 minutes or until lightly browned. Cool.
16 (½-cup) servings

PER SERVING: 205 calories, 12 g total fat (2.5 g saturated fat), 5 g protein, 20 g carbohydrate, 10 mg cholesterol, 330 mg sodium, 2.5 g fiber

Asian Sweet Potato Salad

This tasty salad gets even more interesting when you make it with more than one type of sweet potato. Choose a combination of white-, yellow- and orange-fleshed sweet potatoes (often mislabeled as yams in supermarkets). If your local farmers' market includes vendors selling Asian vegetables, be sure to check them for sweet potato varieties you may not find in supermarkets.

3 lb. sweet potatoes (mixture of white, yellow and orange, if available)
¼ cup plus 1 tablespoon vegetable oil, divided
1 tablespoon minced garlic
1 tablespoon minced fermented black beans or 1½ tablespoons soy sauce

Tortellini Salad with Broccoli, Mushrooms and Tomatoes

1½ tablespoons minced fresh ginger
2 tablespoons rice vinegar
1 tablespoon Dijon mustard
3 green onions, thinly sliced
¾ cup finely diced celery
¼ teaspoon salt
¼ teaspoon freshly ground pepper

1 Pierce sweet potatoes with fork. Cook in batches in microwave on high 6 to 8 minutes or until tender. Let cool; peel. Cut into 1-inch pieces.
2 Meanwhile, heat 1 tablespoon of the oil in small skillet over medium heat. Add garlic, black beans and ginger; cook 2 to 3 minutes or until fragrant, stirring constantly.
3 Remove from heat; whisk in vinegar and mustard. Transfer to large bowl. Whisk in remaining ¼ cup oil. Stir in green onions, celery, salt and pepper. Add sweet potatoes; stir to coat with dressing. Let stand at room temperature 30 minutes.
14 (½-cup) servings

PER SERVING: 125 calories, 5 g total fat (.5 g saturated fat), 2 g protein, 19 g carbohydrate, 0 mg cholesterol, 175 mg sodium, 2 g fiber

Tortellini Salad with Broccoli, Mushrooms and Tomatoes

Summer vegetables shine in this pesto-flavored pasta salad. Substitute other vegetables, if you like, keeping in mind that a variety of colors and textures makes the most pleasing mixture.

4 cups fresh broccoli florets
1 (9-oz.) pkg. refrigerated pesto tortellini
8 tablespoons extra-virgin olive oil, divided
4 oz. small mushrooms, quartered
1 cup pitted ripe olives
1 cup grape or cherry tomatoes
3 garlic cloves, minced
3 tablespoons finely chopped fresh Italian parsley
2 tablespoons chopped fresh basil
½ teaspoon salt
½ teaspoon freshly ground pepper

1 Cook broccoli in large pot of boiling salted water 1 minute or until bright green. Remove from water; reserve water for cooking pasta. Rinse broccoli under cold running water to cool. Place in large bowl.
2 In same large pot of boiling salted water, cook tortellini 3 to 4 minutes or until tender. Drain; toss with 1 tablespoon of the oil. Cool.
3 Add cooled pasta, mushrooms, olives and tomatoes. In small bowl, whisk together remaining 7 tablespoons oil, garlic, parsley, basil, salt and pepper. Pour over pasta mixture. Let stand, covered, at room temperature 2 hours before serving. (Salad can be made up to 1 day ahead. Cover and refrigerate. Bring to room temperature before serving.)
16 (½-cup) servings

PER SERVING: 110 calories, 9 g total fat (1.5 g saturated fat), 2.5 g protein, 6 g carbohydrate, 20 mg cholesterol, 190 mg sodium, 1 g fiber

Beatrice Ojakangas is the author of The Cooking Club of America's *Pure Poultry.*

Grilled Chicken Pasta with Parsley-Chervil Pesto

Chicken with Cumin-Scented Cashew Sauce

Salmon Ravioli

Sweet Potato,
Pork and Sage
Pot Pie

Main Dishes

Panzanella-Stuffed Pork Chops

Salmon and Asparagus en Papillote with Fines Herbes Gremolata

The Finest of Herbs

Four spring herbs lend delicate flavor to seasonal fare.

Text and Recipes by Mary Evans

Like faithful friends, certain herbs return to my northern garden each spring, making themselves useful before their departure to dormancy in the fall. Chives are the first, followed in short order by tarragon. After a trip to the garden center for chervil and parsley, all the elements of the classic French herb combination, fines herbes, are present.

I first learned about fines herbes — a mixture of finely chopped fresh parsley, chives, chervil and tarragon — while taking cooking classes in Paris. These herbs are ideally suited to spring, forming a fresh, spontaneous flavor medley that's at its best when added to delicately seasoned foods at the end of cooking. Each herb brings its own assets and can be used individually or in combination with the others. Chives add subtle onion flavor; chervil shyly bestows a delicate nuance of anise; parsley contributes the essence of fresh green growth; and tarragon offers complexity and zing along with a sweeter anise taste.

The translation of fines herbes best describes the combination: choice, fine or special herbs. Try them and you'll agree.

Salmon and Asparagus en Papillote with Fines Herbes Gremolata

Gremolata is an Italian seasoning made with parsley, garlic and lemon. Here it takes on a French twist with a classic fines herbes mixture.

- 4 (15x12-inch) sheets parchment paper or foil
- 1 tablespoon chopped fresh chives
- 1 tablespoon chopped fresh parsley
- 1 tablespoon chopped fresh tarragon
- 1 tablespoon chopped fresh chervil
- 1 tablespoon chopped fresh garlic chives*
- 1 teaspoon grated lemon peel
- ¼ cup butter, softened
- 1 tablespoon lemon juice
- ¼ teaspoon salt
- ⅛ teaspoon white pepper
- 4 (6-oz.) salmon fillets, skin removed
- 12 to 16 thin asparagus spears, peeled

1 Heat oven to 450°F. Fold parchment sheets in half to form 12x7½-inch rectangles. Cut into half-moon shapes, beginning and ending cutting at folded edges.
2 In small bowl, stir together chives, parsley, tarragon and chervil. Sprinkle 1 teaspoon of the herb mixture on one side of each opened sheet of parchment. Stir garlic chives and lemon peel into remaining herb mixture to make gremolata. In another small bowl, blend butter, lemon juice, salt and pepper to form paste.
3 Place fish on herb-sprinkled side of parchment, parallel to crease. Place one-fourth of the asparagus on each fillet. Place one-fourth of the butter mixture on fish and asparagus. Fold paper over fish and asparagus; crimp and seal edges securely, forming turnover-style packets. Twist and fold ends under securely. Place in 17x12x1-inch pan.
4 Bake 10 to 12 minutes or until packets puff and fish just begins to flake. (Cut slit in one packet to check fish.) To serve in parchment, cut an "X" in top of each packet. Slightly pull back parchment; sprinkle with gremolata.

TIP *Garlic chives are different from the more familiar onion chives in that they are flat, not round, and the tips curl gracefully. They can be used in any recipe calling for chives.
WINE Because this dish has French and Italian heritages, try a wine from either country. Guigal Côtes du Rhône Blanc is very flavorful, while Teruzzi & Puthod Terre di Tufi from Tuscany is an impressively flavored but very subtle dry white.
4 servings

PER SERVING: 320 calories, 20 g total fat (9.5 g saturated fat), 32 g protein, 2 g carbohydrate, 125 mg cholesterol, 310 mg sodium, 1 g fiber

Springtime Herbs

Chervil A cousin of parsley, chervil is the most delicate of the fines herbes components. It has lacy leaves and looks like a fragile version of parsley. Once harvested, it wilts relatively quickly, so use it promptly. When properly stored in a sealed plastic bag in the refrigerator, it keeps for up to three days. To use chervil, remove the lower part of the stem and gently chop or snip the remaining stem and leaves; or pull off the leaves and sprinkle them whole into foods. Add chervil liberally to salads or eggs, or sprinkle it over beets or asparagus.

Tarragon To reappear in spring gardens, this member of the daisy family must go dormant, so it does best in cooler climates. Use tarragon quickly; it keeps refrigerated in a sealed plastic bag no more than four days. Tarragon is one of the foundation herbs of French cooking and its leaves, when chopped, add enormous flavor to mild seafood, fish and chicken. It is a natural paired with vinegar or mustard.

Parsley This kitchen staple comes in two varieties, curly and flat leaf (sometimes called Italian). The flat-leaf parsley has a more pronounced flavor, but use the two interchangeably. Parsley stores well; kept refrigerated in a sealed plastic bag, it lasts at least a week. Remove the leaves from the stem and chop or pinch sprigs for garnish. It is a pleasant complement to almost any savory dish, but the leaves are most effective when added at the end of the cooking process. Add stems to long-cooking dishes, such as soups and stews; remove them before serving.

Chives Each spring, onion chives send up hollow, rounded shoots followed by purple blossoms. Garlic chives have flat shoots and a definite garlic taste. Both varieties can be stored up to a week when refrigerated in a sealed plastic bag. Chop or snip the stems into salads, or add them at the last minute to cheese or egg dishes or as a garnish for soup. The blossoms also make a wonderful garnish, but use them sparingly because they have a much stronger flavor.

Grilled Chicken Pasta with Parsley-Chervil Pesto

Adding crushed fennel sparks the mild anise taste of chervil. Crush the seeds in a mortar and pestle or finely chop them with a sharp knife.

- 1 cup loosely packed fresh Italian parsley
- 1 cup loosely packed fresh chervil
- 1/3 cup chopped fresh chives
- 1/2 cup (2 oz.) freshly grated Parmesan cheese
- 1/4 cup pine nuts
- 1/4 teaspoon crushed fennel seeds
- 1 teaspoon salt, divided
- 1/2 cup buttermilk
- 2 tablespoons extra-virgin olive oil
- 4 boneless skinless chicken breast halves
- 1 teaspoon finely grated lemon peel
- 1/8 teaspoon freshly ground pepper
- 1 yellow bell pepper, halved
- 1 red bell pepper, halved
- 1 (9-oz.) pkg. fresh linguine

1 In food processor, combine parsley, chervil, chives, cheese, pine nuts, fennel seeds and 3/4 teaspoon of the salt. Pulse until paste forms. Add buttermilk and olive oil; pulse to combine.

2 Heat grill. Sprinkle chicken with lemon peel; rub into surface of chicken. Season with remaining 1/4 teaspoon salt and pepper. Place chicken, yellow bell pepper and red bell pepper on gas grill over medium-high heat or on charcoal grill 4 to 6 inches from medium-high coals. Cook 8 to 10 minutes or until peppers are slightly charred, chicken

Grilled Chicken Pasta with Parsley-Chervil Pesto

is no longer pink in center and juices run clear, turning once. Cut peppers into strips.

3 Meanwhile, cook linguine according to package directions. Drain; toss with pesto. Divide among four plates; top each serving with 1 chicken breast and one-fourth of the peppers.

WINE A dry, herbal white wine is perfect with this recipe. Try Casa Lapostolle Sauvignon Blanc from Chile or Grove Mill Sauvignon Blanc from New Zealand.

4 servings

PER SERVING: 540 calories, 20.5 g total fat (5.5 g saturated fat), 41.5 g protein, 48.5 g carbohydrate, 80 mg cholesterol, 1130 mg sodium, 4.5 g fiber

Tarragon-Walnut Chicken Salad

Walnut oil's wonderful nutty taste accentuates the chopped walnuts and acts as a foil for the tarragon. As an alternative, toast the walnuts before chopping them to bring out their flavor, and substitute 2 tablespoons of cream for the walnut oil.

- 4 boneless skinless chicken breast halves
- ¼ cup mayonnaise
- ¼ cup sour cream
- 1 tablespoon tarragon wine vinegar
- ½ teaspoon salt
- ⅛ teaspoon freshly ground pepper
- 2 tablespoons walnut oil
- 2 tablespoons chopped fresh tarragon plus 4 small sprigs
- 1 tablespoon chopped fresh chives
- 1 cup chopped walnuts, divided
- ½ cup chopped dried apricots, divided
- 4 large lettuce leaves

1 Place chicken in large skillet or Dutch oven. Add enough water to cover chicken. Bring to a gentle boil over medium-high heat. Reduce heat to low; simmer 15 minutes or until no longer pink in center and juices run clear. Remove chicken from liquid. Cool; cut into ½-inch cubes.

2 In small bowl, blend together mayonnaise and sour cream; stir in vinegar, salt and pepper. Whisk in walnut oil until blended. Stir in chopped tarragon and chives. Reserve 2 tablespoons of the walnuts and 2 tablespoons of the apricots for garnish; add remainder to mayonnaise mixture. Mix well. Stir in chicken. Cover and refrigerate 1 to 2 hours or until well chilled.

3 Place 1 lettuce leaf on each plate; mound chicken salad onto leaves. Sprinkle with reserved walnuts and apricots; garnish with tarragon sprigs.

WINE There are lots of nutty, herbal flavors in this dish, so choose a wine with similar nuances. Guigal Côtes du Rhône Blanc from France or Murphy-Goode Reserve Fumé Blanc from Sonoma pairs beautifully with this salad.

4 servings

PER SERVING: 565 calories, 42.5 g total fat (6.5 g saturated fat), 32 g protein, 17.5 g carbohydrate, 85 mg cholesterol, 440 mg sodium, 3.5 g fiber

Pork Tenderloin with Tarragon-Mustard Sauce

Crème fraîche is an ideal ingredient choice when higher heat is used. Unlike sour cream, it will not curdle when boiled or baked.

- ¼ cup crème fraîche or whipping cream
- ¼ cup Dijon mustard
- 2 tablespoons minced fresh tarragon
- 2 (¾-lb.) pork tenderloins
- ¼ teaspoon salt
- ⅛ teaspoon freshly ground pepper
- 1 tablespoon canola oil
- ½ cup white wine

1 Heat oven to 400°F. In small bowl, stir together crème fraîche, mustard and tarragon.

2 Sprinkle pork tenderloins with salt and pepper. Heat large skillet over medium-high heat until hot. Add oil; heat until hot. Cook pork 4 to 6 minutes or until browned, turning once. Place pork in shallow roasting pan.

3 Place same skillet over high heat. Add wine; bring to a boil, scraping up browned bits from bottom of skillet. Pour wine mixture around pork in roasting pan. Brush pork with 2 tablespoons of the mustard mixture. Bake 15 to 25 minutes or until internal temperature reaches 145°F. Place on serving platter; cover loosely with foil.

4 Place roasting pan over low heat. Whisk remaining mustard mixture into pan juices. Slice tenderloin into medallions; pour sauce over pork.

BEER/WINE To pick up on the spicy sauce, you can try either a spicy beer, such as Sierra Nevada Pale Ale, or a Gewürztraminer: The Lorentz from Alsace has spice as well as a beautiful floral aroma.

6 servings

PER SERVING: 210 calories, 10 g total fat (3.5 g saturated fat), 26.5 g protein, 1.5 g carbohydrate, 85 mg cholesterol, 285 mg sodium, .5 g fiber

Triple-Cream Cheese

Triple-cream cheese, such as that called for in *Souffléed Omelet with Fines Herbes*, is an exceptionally rich and creamy — almost velvety — soft cheese. Its richness comes from the cream that is used, along with milk, to make the cheese. It contains at least 75 percent butterfat, compared to 45 to 50 percent butterfat in other soft cheeses and 60 percent butterfat in double-cream cheese. Some well-known triple creams are St. André, Brillat-Savarin, Explorateur and Boursin. If necessary, you can substitute another flavorful soft cheese, such as Brie, Rondelé or soft goat cheese.

Souffléed Omelet with Fines Herbes

For a lighter dish, omit the cheese and add cooked asparagus pieces to the filling instead.

- 1 tablespoon minced fresh chervil plus 1 tablespoon fresh chervil leaves
- 1 tablespoon minced fresh chives
- 1 tablespoon minced fresh parsley
- 1 tablespoon minced fresh tarragon
- 4 eggs
- 4 egg yolks
- ¼ teaspoon salt
- ⅛ teaspoon freshly ground pepper
- 4 egg whites
- ½ teaspoon cream of tartar
- 2 tablespoons butter
- 4 oz. mild French triple-cream cheese (such as St. André), rind removed, cut up

Souffléed Omelet with Fines Herbes

1 Heat oven to 375°F. In small bowl, stir together minced chervil, chives, parsley and tarragon.

2 Beat eggs and egg yolks in medium bowl at medium speed 3 to 4 minutes or until almost tripled in volume. Stir in 1 tablespoon of the herb mixture, salt and pepper.

3 Beat egg whites in another medium bowl at medium speed until frothy; beat in cream of tartar. Increase speed to high; beat until soft peaks form. (Tips of whites will dip slightly when beater is raised.) Stir one-fourth of the egg whites into egg yolk mixture; fold in remaining whites.

4 Immediately melt butter in large (12-inch) ovenproof nonstick skillet over medium-high heat until foamy, swirling to coat sides. Pour in egg mixture; cook over medium to medium-low heat 1 minute. Place in oven; bake 7 to 9 minutes or until eggs are just set. Top with cheese and remaining herb mixture. Fold omelet in half; slide onto serving platter. Sprinkle with chervil leaves. Serve immediately.

4 servings

PER SERVING: 300 calories, 25.5 g total fat (13 g saturated fat), 15 g protein, 2.5 g carbohydrate, 470 mg cholesterol, 395 mg sodium, 0 g fiber

Mary Evans is the author of The Cooking Club of America's *Vegetable Creations.*

Rosemary-Fennel Roasted Pork Loin

Company's Coming

The focus is on comfort in this heartwarming holiday menu.

Recipes by Janice Cole and Alice Medrich

Nothing says "Welcome" during the holidays more warmly than a home filled with delicious aromas. And when the food tastes as good as the aromas suggest, you have the recipe for a perfect evening to share with guests.

This menu takes its cue from the kinds of foods we're craving these days: dishes that are comforting and familiar. But it goes a step further with ingredients and flavors that give each recipe a fresh twist. A warm cheese salad gets a kick from Gorgonzola, a roasted pork loin is studded with fragrant rosemary and garlic, and scalloped potatoes take a rich, earthy turn with wild mushrooms. There's only one ending that's fitting for a meal this satisfying — a decadent chocolate cake. Cocoa-rich with a hint of coffee, it's the perfect way to cap a night of friendship.

Rosemary-Fennel Roasted Pork Loin

Butchers often tie two pork loins together, one on top of the other, and place them in netting for a pork loin roast. For this recipe, however, ask for a single pork loin; it will roast more quickly and evenly.

- 2½ lb. boneless pork loin
- 4 large garlic cloves, minced
- 2 tablespoons chopped fresh rosemary
- 3 tablespoons olive oil
- 1 teaspoon kosher (coarse) salt
- 1 teaspoon freshly ground pepper
- 8 large shallots, quartered
- 3 fennel bulbs, fronds removed and discarded, cut into 1-inch wedges
- 2 carrots, sliced diagonally (¼ inch)
- ½ cup red wine

1 Heat oven to 450°F. Grease 17x11-inch rimmed baking sheet. Place pork in center. With tip of small sharp knife, make 1-inch slits in top and sides of pork. In small bowl, combine garlic, rosemary, 2 tablespoons of the olive oil, salt and pepper. Coat pork loin with half of the rosemary mixture, pushing some of the mixture into slits.

2 In large bowl, toss shallots, fennel, carrots and remaining 1 tablespoon olive oil with remaining rosemary mixture. Place vegetables around pork. Bake 15 minutes. Reduce temperature to 400°F.; bake 25 to 35 minutes or until internal temperature of pork registers 145°F. Place pork on serving platter; cover loosely with foil. Let stand 15 to 20 minutes. Meanwhile, return vegetables to oven; continue baking 5 to 10 minutes or until tender.

3 Place vegetables on serving platter. Place baking sheet over medium-high heat. Add wine; bring to a boil. Boil 1 to 2 minutes, stirring to scrape up browned bits from bottom of pan. Simmer, stirring occasionally, 1 minute. Serve pork with pan juices.

WINE Try a spicy red with this dish, which will pick up on the flavor of the fennel. Trapiche Malbec from Argentina and Dry Creek Old Vines Zinfandel are ideal.

6 servings

PER SERVING: 435 calories, 22 g total fat (6 g saturated fat), 44.5 g protein, 15 g carbohydrate, 120 mg cholesterol, 410 mg sodium, 5 g fiber

Warm Gorgonzola-Walnut Salad

Watch the cheese carefully while it bakes. It should be soft and just
beginning to melt but should not be runny.

SALAD

- 4 oz. Gorgonzola cheese
- 3 tablespoons honey, warm
- ½ cup panko, toasted*
- 8 cups mixed salad greens
- ¼ cup sliced green onions
- ½ cup walnuts, toasted**
- ½ cup pomegranate seeds

DRESSING

- 1½ tablespoons sherry or red wine vinegar
- 1½ teaspoons Dijon mustard
- ¼ teaspoon kosher (coarse) salt
- ¼ teaspoon freshly ground pepper
- ¼ cup walnut oil

1 Cut cheese into 6 equal pieces. (If cheese is difficult to cut with knife, try using unflavored dental floss.) Brush honey over cheese; coat with panko. Place on greased baking sheet; freeze 1 hour or refrigerate 2 hours.

2 Meanwhile, in small bowl, whisk together sherry vinegar, mustard, salt and pepper. Slowly whisk in oil.

3 When ready to serve, heat oven to 475°F. Bake cheese 3 to 5 minutes or until just beginning to melt. While cheese is baking, in large bowl, toss salad greens and green onions with dressing. Place on individual salad plates. Top with warm cheese; sprinkle with walnuts and pomegranate seeds. Serve immediately.

TIPS *Panko, a coarser Japanese-style bread crumb, is usually found next to other bread crumbs in the supermarket. Toast panko on rimmed baking sheet at 375°F. for 4 to 6 minutes or until light brown, stirring occasionally.

**To toast walnuts, spread on baking sheet; bake at 375°F. for 7 to 10 minutes or until lightly browned. Cool.

6 servings

PER SERVING: 300 calories, 20.5 g total fat (5 g saturated fat), 8 g protein, 24 g carbohydrate, 15 mg cholesterol, 445 mg sodium, 3.5 g fiber

Wild Mushroom-Potato Gratin

Dried mushrooms add intense flavor to this take-off on scalloped potatoes.

 1 oz. dried porcini or shiitake mushrooms (about 1 cup)
 1 tablespoon butter
 2 large garlic cloves, minced
 2 cups whipping cream
 ¾ teaspoon salt
 ¼ teaspoon freshly ground pepper
 2 lb. Yukon Gold potatoes (about 5 medium), peeled, thinly sliced (¼ inch)
 ¼ cup (1 oz.) shredded Asiago cheese

1 Place mushrooms in small bowl; cover with hot water. Let stand 20 to 30 minutes or until softened. Drain, reserving ¼ cup mushroom liquid. Rinse mushrooms under water to remove any sediment. If using shiitakes, remove and discard stems. Slice mushrooms.

2 Heat oven to 400°F. Spray 6-cup gratin or 8x8-inch baking dish with nonstick cooking spray. In large saucepan, melt butter over medium heat. Add garlic; cook 30 to 40 seconds or until fragrant. Stir in mushrooms, cream, ¼ cup reserved mushroom liquid, salt and pepper. Add potatoes. Bring to a boil, stirring

occasionally. Reduce heat to low; simmer 5 minutes.

3 Carefully spoon mixture into gratin dish. (Recipe can be made to this point up to 24 hours ahead. Cover and refrigerate. Baking time may need to be increased 5 to 10 minutes.) Sprinkle with cheese. Bake 30 to 35 minutes or until potatoes are tender and sauce has thickened. Let stand 10 minutes.

6 servings

PER SERVING: 390 calories, 28 g total fat (17.5 g saturated fat), 6 g protein, 31 g carbohydrate, 100 mg cholesterol, 350 mg sodium, 2.5 g fiber

Decadent Dark Chocolate Cake

This is the ultimate chocolate cake, perfect for entertaining — or anytime! Top it with the beautiful, satiny chocolate glaze or simply sprinkle it with powdered sugar. Be sure to use Dutch-process cocoa; natural cocoa will not work.

CAKE
 1 cup all-purpose flour
 ½ cup unsweetened Dutch-process cocoa
 ½ teaspoon salt
 ¼ teaspoon baking powder
 ¼ teaspoon baking soda
 ½ cup buttermilk, room temperature
 2 teaspoons instant espresso coffee powder
 1 teaspoon vanilla
10 tablespoons unsalted butter, softened
 1⅓ cups sugar
 3 eggs, room temperature, beaten

GLAZE
 3 tablespoons unsalted butter
 ⅓ cup whipping cream
 ⅓ cup sugar
 ⅓ cup unsweetened Dutch-process cocoa
    Pinch salt
 ½ teaspoon vanilla

1 Heat oven to 350°F. Spray 6-cup (8½-inch) kugelhopf pan with nonstick cooking spray.* In large bowl, combine flour, ½ cup cocoa,

Decadent Dark Chocolate Cake

½ teaspoon salt, baking powder and baking soda. Sift; set aside.

2 In medium bowl, combine buttermilk, coffee powder and 1 teaspoon vanilla; stir until coffee is dissolved.

3 In large bowl, beat 10 tablespoons butter at medium speed until creamy. Slowly add 1⅓ cups sugar. Increase speed to medium-high; beat 4 to 5 minutes or until light and fluffy. Reduce speed to medium; slowly add eggs to butter mixture, beating constantly. (This should take 2½ to 3 minutes.)

4 Alternately add flour mixture and buttermilk mixture, beginning and ending with flour mixture, beating at low speed only enough to incorporate ingredients after each addition, scraping bowl as necessary. Spread batter evenly in pan.

5 Bake 45 to 55 minutes or until toothpick inserted in center comes out clean. Cool cake in pan on wire rack 10 minutes. Invert cake onto wire rack; cool completely. (Cake can be prepared to this point, covered and kept at room temperature 4 to 5 days. Or freeze up to 3 months.)

6 Melt 3 tablespoons butter in medium saucepan. Add cream, 1/3 cup sugar, 1/3 cup cocoa and dash salt; mix well. Cook over medium heat until mixture is smooth and hot but not boiling, whisking constantly. Remove from heat; stir in 1/2 teaspoon vanilla. Refrigerate 15 to 20 minutes or until slightly thickened.

7 Place cooled cake on rack over baking sheet. Pour glaze over cake. Let stand until firm. (Store any leftover glaze in refrigerator for another use; reheat gently in saucepan over barely simmering water or in microwave before using.)

TIP *Cake also can be made in 11x7-inch glass baking dish. Bake 40 to 45 minutes.

12 servings

PER SERVING: 465 calories, 26 g total fat (15.5 g saturated fat), 6 g protein, 58 g carbohydrate, 130 mg cholesterol, 230 mg sodium, 3.5 g fiber

Janice Cole is *Cooking Pleasures* food editor. Alice Medrich is the author of *A Year in Chocolate* (Warner Books).

Honey Mustard-Crusted Salmon

A Touch of Mustard

Deftly used, this potent ingredient adds a subtle tang to your cooking.

Text and Recipes by Melanie Barnard

Mustard has always been a fundamental and integral part of the world's major cuisines. French, Chinese, Japanese, English and Indian cooking rely heavily on it, though each favors its own particular style and preparation. The French love their creamy Dijon from the house of Poupon, but they also favor the grainy Moutard de Meaux for cooking. The British are best known for the unique dry mustard concocted by Jeremiah Colman of Norwich, still sold today under the Colman name. The Chinese use dry and prepared mustard freely, while Indian cooking highlights whole mustard seeds in many classic dishes.

With so many choices, mustard can be an ingredient with enormous potential in American kitchens. Once you become familiar with the varieties and their levels of potency, it's easy to adapt mustard to your personal tastes. A little dab transforms the simplest recipe into a tasteful triumph.

Honey Mustard-Crusted Salmon

Roasting at high heat keeps the fish moist and flavorful. The combination of honey mustard and whole mustard seeds produces a lovely hot-sweet mustard flavor. Salmon steaks can be substituted for fillets.

- 1 (1¾- to 2-lb.) salmon fillet
- ¼ cup honey mustard
- 2 tablespoons butter, melted
- 2 tablespoons chopped fresh dill
- 1 tablespoon lemon juice
- 1 teaspoon whole mustard seeds, lightly crushed
- ¼ teaspoon freshly ground pepper
  Lemon wedges
  Dill sprigs

1 Heat oven to 475°F. Grease rimmed baking sheet. Place salmon, skin side down, on baking sheet. In small bowl, stir together honey mustard, butter, chopped dill, lemon juice, mustard seeds and pepper. Spread over salmon.
2 Bake salmon 10 to 12 minutes or until fish just begins to flake. Heat broiler. Broil 3 to 4 inches from heat 1 minute or until lightly browned.
3 Slice salmon into 6 pieces; garnish with lemon wedges and dill sprigs.

WINE Chardonnay is a good choice with this dish. Try Lindemans Bin 65 from Australia or Rodney Strong "Chalk Hill" from Sonoma, which has a subtle spiciness.
6 servings

PER SERVING: 250 calories, 11.5 g total fat (4.5 g saturated fat), 28.5 g protein, 5 g carbohydrate, 95 mg cholesterol, 115 mg sodium, .5 g fiber

Cheddar-Ale Soup

Add a spinach or romaine salad and some crusty bread for a simple, warming winter supper. Or serve the soup in small bowls or cups as a prelude to a meal for company. You may garnish the soup with crumbled bacon or diced ham, or add nearly any other cooked vegetable, from artichoke hearts to zucchini, as a flavorful variation.

- ¼ cup butter
- 1 cup coarsely chopped onion
- 1 cup coarsely chopped celery
- 1 cup coarsely chopped carrot
- 6 tablespoons all-purpose flour
- 4 teaspoons dry English mustard (such as Colman's)
- 3½ cups reduced-sodium chicken broth
- 12 oz. flat ale or beer
- 1½ cups half-and-half or milk
- 4 cups (1 lb.) finely shredded cheddar cheese
- ½ cup thinly sliced purchased roasted red bell peppers
- 2 teaspoons Worcestershire sauce

1 In heavy large saucepan, melt butter over medium heat. Add onion, celery and carrot; cook 10 to 15 minutes or just until softened, stirring often. Add flour and mustard. Cook and stir 1 minute. Slowly stir in broth and ale. Bring to a boil, stirring constantly. Reduce heat to medium. Add half-and-half; simmer 2 minutes.
2 Remove pan from heat. Add cheese 1 cup at a time, stirring gently to melt each cup before adding the next. Stir in roasted peppers and Worcestershire sauce. Serve immediately. (Soup can be made up to 2 days ahead. Cover and refrigerate.)
6 (1½-cup) servings

PER SERVING: 550 calories, 41 g total fat (25.5 g saturated fat), 25.5 g protein, 18.5 g carbohydrate, 120 mg cholesterol, 870 mg sodium, 2 g fiber

Pan-Seared Mustard-Peppercorn Steak with Mushroom Sauce

Pan-Seared Mustard-Peppercorn Steak with Mushroom Sauce

Any tender beefsteak can be used in this recipe. For the best flavor and most mustard coating per bite, the steaks should be no less than 3/4 inch thick. Jars containing a mixture of green, black and white peppercorns are available in the spice section of many markets.

- 1 oz. dried porcini or shiitake mushrooms (about 1 cup)
- 2 teaspoons multicolored peppercorns
- 2 teaspoons whole mustard seeds
- 3/4 teaspoon kosher (coarse) salt, divided
- 4 boneless New York strip steaks (3/4 inch thick)*
- 3 tablespoons butter, divided
- 1/4 cup chopped shallots
- 1/4 cup red wine or mushroom soaking liquid
- 1 tablespoon coarse-grain Dijon mustard

1 Place mushrooms in small bowl; cover with boiling water. Let stand 20 to 30 minutes or until softened. Drain well, reserving 1/4 cup liquid. (If using mushroom liquid in place of wine, reserve 1/2 cup liquid.) If using shiitakes, remove and discard stems.

2 Place peppercorns in heavy-duty plastic bag; coarsely crush with flat side of meat mallet. Add mustard seeds; crush slightly. Mix in 1/2 teaspoon of the salt. Firmly press peppercorn mixture onto both sides of steaks.

3 In large skillet, heat 2 tablespoons of the butter over medium-high heat until melted. Add steaks; cook 5 to 7 minutes for medium-rare or until of desired doneness, turning once. Place steaks on serving platter; loosely

cover with foil to keep warm.

4 In same skillet, melt remaining 1 tablespoon butter over medium heat. Add shallots; cook 1 minute. Add mushrooms; cook 1 minute. Add wine, 1/4 cup reserved mushroom liquid, mustard and remaining 1/4 teaspoon salt. Cook 2 to 3 minutes or until liquid is slightly reduced, stirring often. Add any juices from steaks to skillet. If necessary, return steaks to skillet 1 to 2 minutes to reheat.

TIP *New York strip steaks are also called loin, Kansas City or strip steaks.

WINE This dish needs a hearty, spicy red to stand up to all of its flavors. Rosemount "Diamond" Shiraz from Australia works well, as does Clos du Bois Reserve Shiraz from Sonoma.

4 servings

PER SERVING: 365 calories, 21.5 g total fat (10 g saturated fat), 38 g protein, 3 g carbohydrate, 120 mg cholesterol, 490 mg sodium, 1 g fiber

About Mustard

Mustard is used in several forms in cooking: whole seeds, dry and prepared.

Whole Seeds There are just two types of mustard seeds produced commercially, brown and yellow (also called white). Canada is the world's leading grower and exporter. Most mustard seeds sold in supermarkets are the yellow variety, but you can get the smaller brown seeds from specialty stores or by mail order. Most prepared mustard is made from these two seeds. In cooking, to release their flavor, whole seeds are typically crushed or heated in oil until they pop. Mustard seeds can be stored indefinitely on a cool, dry, dark pantry shelf.

Dry Mustard This is nothing more than the ground powder of yellow or brown mustard seeds. Most commercial dry mustard comes from yellow seeds. There is actually very little difference between pure dry mustards; so, for example, the well-known British Colman's is generally interchangeable with Chinese dry mustard. Remember that, as with any ground spice, dry mustard is less shelf-stable than mustard seeds. It should be replaced at least once a year for maximum potency.

Prepared Mustard This is where mustard gets personality. The preparation and added ingredients give a mustard its character. Most cooks are familiar with the yellow ballpark mustard (which gets it color from turmeric and not mustard) and the Americanized version of French Dijon mustard. But there are many other varieties, from garlic mustard to raspberry mustard to curry mustard.

Prepared mustards are made by reconstituting mustard powder or pulverizing seeds, then adding flavors and sometimes color. In some parts of the world, prepared mustard is made fresh by home cooks, but in the United States there are more than 700 varieties made by various producers. Although it is safe on the pantry shelf, an opened container of prepared mustard should be stored in the refrigerator to preserve the flavor.

Cooking Mustard's pungency comes from an essential oil that forms when ground seeds are mixed with cold water. Heat and strong acid diminish and can even destroy the developing mustard enzyme, so avoid cooking dry mustard or pulverized seeds for long periods of time. Either mix with cold water and let stand for at least 10 minutes before using as a prepared mustard, or add to a recipe near the end of the cooking time, and avoid adding with acids. Conversely, prepared mustard is quite stable and, in fact, is a classic emulsifier for vinaigrette and mayonnaise.

Roasted Game Hens with Apricot-Mustard Glaze

Roasted Game Hens with Apricot-Mustard Glaze

Mustard and fruit have a natural affinity. If you don't have apricot preserves, try peach preserves or orange marmalade. This versatile recipe works just as well with bone-in chicken breasts, legs or thighs, or duck breasts.

- 2 Cornish game hens (about 1½ lb. each), cut in half*
- ½ teaspoon salt, divided
- ½ teaspoon freshly ground pepper, divided
- ⅓ cup apricot preserves
- ⅔ cup white wine, divided
- 2 teaspoons dry mustard
- ⅓ cup diced dried apricots

1 Heat oven to 450°F. Season hens with ¼ teaspoon each of the salt and pepper. Place, skin side up, on 15x10x1-inch pan. Bake 15 minutes.
2 Meanwhile, in small saucepan, stir together preserves, ⅓ cup of the wine, mustard and remaining ¼ teaspoon each of the salt and pepper. Let stand 10 minutes. Bring to a simmer over medium-low heat; simmer 2 minutes or until mustard is dissolved. Reserve half of the glaze.
3 Brush roasted hens with reserved glaze. Bake hens an additional 20 minutes or until rich golden brown and no longer pink in center, brushing once or twice with reserved glaze.
4 While hens are roasting, add remaining ⅓ cup wine and apricots to glaze in saucepan. Bring to a simmer over medium-low heat; simmer 5 minutes or until apricots are tender. Spoon sauce over hens.
TIP *Use kitchen shears to cut game hens in half. Cut on either side of backbone and through breast bone into halves.
WINE A rich, fruit-driven white that doesn't overpower the hens is a good choice here. Try Casa Lapostolle Chardonnay from Chile or Byron Chardonnay from Santa Maria, California, with its tropical fruit flavors.
4 servings

PER SERVING: 400 calories, 21.5 g total fat (6 g saturated fat), 26.5 g protein, 24.5 g carbohydrate, 150 mg cholesterol, 380 mg sodium, 1.5 g fiber

Chinese Mustard and Sesame-Glazed Pork Tenderloin

Chinese mustard adds a delightful hot bite to the very tasty sesame-ginger glaze. Serve the pork with a colorful vegetable stir-fry.

- 2 tablespoons plus 1 teaspoon prepared Chinese mustard, divided
- 1 tablespoon dark sesame oil
- 1 tablespoon minced fresh ginger
- 1 teaspoon soy sauce
- 2 (¾-lb.) pork tenderloins
- 2 tablespoons sesame seeds, toasted*
- 3 tablespoons dry sherry, divided
- ⅓ cup reduced-sodium chicken broth

1 Heat oven to 450°F. In small dish, stir together 2 tablespoons of the mustard, sesame oil, ginger and soy sauce. Cover pork with mustard mixture; sprinkle on all sides with sesame seeds.
2 Place pork in shallow roasting pan; drizzle with 1 tablespoon of the sherry. Cook 25 to 30 minutes or until internal temperature reaches 145°F. Transfer to platter; let stand 5 to 10 minutes.
3 Meanwhile, place roasting pan over medium-high heat. Stir in broth, remaining 2 tablespoons sherry and remaining 1 teaspoon mustard. Bring to a boil, stirring to scrape up browned bits from bottom of pan. Reduce heat to medium-low; simmer, stirring, 1 minute.
4 Slice pork diagonally; serve with pan sauce.
TIP *To toast sesame seeds, heat dry small skillet over medium heat. Add sesame seeds; cook 3 to 4 minutes or until seeds are lightly browned, stirring constantly.
WINE A Gewürztraminer picks up on the spiciness of this dish while helping to tone down the heat from the mustard. Try Alexander Valley Vineyards from Sonoma or Trimbach from Alsace.
6 servings

PER SERVING: 190 calories, 8 g total fat (2 g saturated fat), 25.5 g protein, 2 g carbohydrate, 65 mg cholesterol, 205 mg sodium, .5 g fiber

Melanie Barnard is a Connecticut-based food writer.

Chicken with Cumin-Scented Cashew Sauce

The Spice Factor

Create several flavors from one spice — by roasting, toasting, grinding and more.

Text and Recipes by Raghavan Iyer

When it comes to exploring the potential of spices, Indian cooks are the masters. I should know. I grew up in India where I watched my mother create magic in the kitchen as she extracted multiple flavors and aromas from a single spice.

Today, as a cooking teacher and author, I'm sharing what I learned at my mother's side: Spices are like chameleons; their flavors and aromas can change with the smallest prompting.

Grind a spice from its whole form and it perfumes the air. Toast a whole spice and it takes on a nutty aroma. With these and other simple techniques, you can alter the character of a spice — and the dish you're creating. You'll discover that the richness and layers of taste within any given dish need not come from 50 ingredients — they can come from a single spice with several personalities.

Chicken with Cumin-Scented Cashew Sauce

This recipe is a perfect example of how complex flavors can be derived from the same spice if used in different ways: cumin seed sautéed in oil versus cumin seed dry-roasted in a skillet and then ground. The blackening of chiles imparts a wonderful pungency with a slight smokiness.

- 4 large garlic cloves, unpeeled
- 2 serrano chiles
- 1/4 cup whipping cream
- 1 1/2 teaspoons salt, divided
- 4 boneless skinless chicken breast halves
- 2 teaspoons cumin seeds, divided
- 2 tablespoons vegetable oil, divided
- 1/2 cup chopped raw cashews*
- 1/2 cup water
- 1 medium red onion, halved, thinly sliced
- 1 medium tomato, finely chopped
- 2 tablespoons finely chopped fresh cilantro

1 Heat small nonstick skillet over medium heat until hot. Add garlic and chiles; cook 10 to 12 minutes or until garlic skins blacken and chiles blister and turn black, turning occasionally. Remove from pan; let stand 3 to 5 minutes or until cool enough to handle. Peel and discard charred garlic skins. Place garlic and chiles in food processor; process until finely minced.

2 In medium bowl, stir together garlic mixture, cream and 1 teaspoon of the salt. Add chicken breasts; turn to coat. Cover and refrigerate at least 1 hour or overnight.

3 Meanwhile, place 1 teaspoon of the cumin seeds in dry heavy small skillet over medium-high heat. Cook 1 minute or until seeds turn reddish brown and become fragrant, shaking pan occasionally or stirring with spoon. Cool; finely grind with mortar and pestle or in spice grinder.

4 Heat 1 tablespoon of the oil in medium skillet over medium-high heat. Add cashews; cook 2 minutes or until golden brown, stirring occasionally. In blender, combine cashews, water, remaining 1/2 teaspoon salt and roasted ground cumin; blend until smooth.

5 In same medium skillet, heat remaining 1 tablespoon oil over medium-high heat. Add remaining 1 teaspoon cumin seeds; cook 10 to 15 seconds or until fragrant. Add onion; cook 3 to 5 minutes or until onion turns light brown, stirring occasionally. Stir in tomato; cook an additional 1 to 2 minutes or just until warm. Stir in cilantro.

6 Heat broiler; lightly spray broiler pan with nonstick cooking spray. Broil chicken breasts 4 to 6 inches from heat 8 to 12 minutes or until juices run clear, turning once.

7 Transfer chicken to serving platter. Spoon cashew sauce over chicken; top with tomato-onion mixture.

TIP *If raw cashews are not available, use roasted cashews and omit cooking cashews in 1 tablespoon oil.

4 servings

PER SERVING: 380 calories, 23.5 g total fat (6.5 g saturated fat), 30.5 g protein, 13 g carbohydrate, 85 mg cholesterol, 950 mg sodium, 2 g fiber

Pork Tenderloin Roast with Whole Spices

Pork Tenderloin Roast with Whole Spices

Coriander is rarely used in its whole form because of its sharp flavor when bitten into. But when it's rubbed into meat and then roasted, as it is here, its flavor mellows considerably. This recipe demonstrates how you can achieve two starkly different tastes from the same spice (whole, roasted coriander and ground coriander). The result is delicious.

3 tablespoons olive oil, divided
2 (¾-lb.) pork tenderloins
1 tablespoon coriander seeds

1 teaspoon cumin seeds
6 medium garlic cloves, minced
1½ teaspoons salt, divided
2 tablespoons finely chopped fresh cilantro, divided
1 tablespoon coriander seeds, ground
1 teaspoon cumin seeds, ground
½ teaspoon cayenne pepper
1 large Granny Smith apple, cut into ½-inch pieces
1 medium russet potato, peeled, cut into ½-inch pieces
1 small sweet potato, cut into ½-inch pieces*

1 Heat oven to 375°F. Heat 1

tablespoon of the oil in large skillet over medium-high heat. Add pork; cook 3 to 4 minutes or until brown on all sides, turning occasionally. Remove from skillet; place in shallow roasting pan. When cool to the touch, make 1-inch-deep diagonal cuts, about 1½ inches apart, in pork.
2 In small bowl, combine 1 tablespoon of the oil, 1 tablespoon coriander seeds, 1 teaspoon cumin seeds, garlic, 1 teaspoon of the salt and 1 tablespoon of the cilantro; fill cuts in pork with mixture.
3 In medium bowl, combine ground coriander seeds, ground cumin seeds, cayenne pepper, and remaining 1

tablespoon oil, 1 tablespoon cilantro and $\frac{1}{2}$ teaspoon salt. Add apple, potato and sweet potato; toss to combine. Spread mixture around pork.

4 Bake 20 minutes or until internal temperature of pork reaches 145°F. Remove pork from roasting pan; place on serving platter. Cover loosely with foil. Return vegetables to oven; bake an additional 10 minutes or until fork-tender. Slice pork $\frac{1}{2}$ inch thick. Place vegetables on serving platter around pork.

TIP *Look for the deep orange-colored sweet potatoes, often labeled as yams.

WINE The deliciously fruity Bonny Doon Pacific Rim Dry Reisling complements the fruit flavors of this pork. Another option is the floral Michel Torino Don David Torrontés Reserve, a tropical beauty from Argentina.

6 servings

PER SERVING: 260 calories, 11.5 g total fat (2.5 g saturated fat), 25 g protein, 14.5 g carbohydrate, 65 mg cholesterol, 635 mg sodium, 2 g fiber

Orzo with Arugula and Red Beans

Toasted ground coriander and cumin are the basis of this dish's robust flavor. Grind the spices in a spice grinder until the texture looks like that of ground black pepper. If you wish, you can substitute mustard greens for the arugula. Sauté them until tender.

- 2 tablespoons olive oil
- 1 medium onion, finely chopped
- 1 tablespoon coriander seeds, ground
- 1 teaspoon cumin seeds, ground
- 1 teaspoon cayenne pepper
- $\frac{1}{2}$ teaspoon salt
- 2 tablespoons finely chopped fresh cilantro
- 1 (15-oz.) can kidney beans, drained, rinsed
- 2 cups vegetable broth
- 1 lb. arugula, stems removed and discarded, leaves coarsely chopped
- 2 cups orzo

1 Heat oil in large saucepan over medium-high heat until hot. Add onion; cook 5 to 7 minutes or until onion begins to brown, stirring occasionally. Stir in coriander, cumin, cayenne pepper and salt; cook 1 to 2 minutes or until fragrant, stirring occasionally.

2 Add cilantro, beans and broth; bring to a boil. Reduce heat to low; simmer, uncovered, about 5 minutes to blend flavors. Add arugula; cook 1 minute or until just wilted.

3 Meanwhile, cook orzo according to package directions. Add to bean mixture; toss well.

4 servings

PER SERVING: 415 calories, 9 g total fat (1 g saturated fat), 15.5 g protein, 69.5 g carbohydrate, 0 mg cholesterol, 1305 mg sodium, 7 g fiber

Shrimp with Papaya and Peppers

This recipe accents the stronger flavors that can be achieved when coriander seed and dried chiles are toasted and ground. The chiles' hot character is especially heightened when dry-roasted. The uncooked, toasted rice also imparts a delicate nuttiness to the dish. Use scallops (or a combination of shrimp and scallops) for an equally delicious alternative. If papaya is unavailable, fresh mangoes offer an interesting substitute.

- 1 tablespoon coriander seeds
- 1 tablespoon rice
- 1 to 2 dried Thai or cayenne chiles
- 1 teaspoon salt, divided
- 1 lb. shelled, deveined uncooked jumbo shrimp
- 2 tablespoons vegetable oil, divided
- 1 teaspoon cumin seeds
- 2 cups diced red, green and/or yellow bell peppers ($\frac{1}{2}$ inch)
- 1 cup chopped papaya ($\frac{1}{2}$ inch)
- 1 tablespoon finely chopped fresh cilantro

Hot Stuff

When you mince chiles with onion and then stir-fry the combination, the chiles' inherent heat is remarkably masked. Even though the fumes escaping the saucepan are throat-constricting and pungent (use adequate ventilation), the end result is surprisingly mellow in flavor.

1 Heat small skillet over medium-high heat until hot; add coriander seeds, rice and chiles. Cook 2 to 3 minutes or until fragrant, seeds and rice turn reddish brown and chiles blacken slightly, stirring occasionally; cool. Grind in spice grinder until mixture is texture of finely ground pepper.

2 In medium bowl, stir together spice blend, $\frac{1}{2}$ teaspoon of the salt and shrimp; cover and refrigerate at least 1 hour or overnight.

3 In large skillet, heat 1 tablespoon of the oil over medium-high heat until hot. Add shrimp in single layer; cook 2 to 4 minutes or until shrimp just begin to turn pink, turning once. Remove from skillet.

4 Wipe skillet; heat remaining 1 tablespoon oil over medium-high heat. Add cumin seeds; cook 10 to 15 seconds or until fragrant. Immediately add bell peppers; cook an additional 2 minutes.

5 Add shrimp, papaya, cilantro and remaining $\frac{1}{2}$ teaspoon salt; cook an additional 2 to 3 minutes or until shrimp turn pink and papaya is hot.

WINE/BEER Try Eyrie Pinot Gris Estate for its ripe flavors and good structure. Or opt for a cool, refreshing beer, such as Foster's Lager, with its complex, slightly bitter flavors and full body.

4 servings

PER SERVING: 185 calories, 8 g total fat (1.5 g saturated fat), 18.5 g protein, 10 g carbohydrate, 160 mg cholesterol, 770 mg sodium, 2 g fiber

One Spice, Six Flavors

The beauty of many spices is their ability to provide up to six distinct flavors. For the best flavors and variety of tastes, you must start with whole spices. Even if the dish you're making requires ground spice, you'll get fresher, stronger flavors if you grind the spice as you need it. Each of the following techniques yields a different flavor and can be used with a wide variety of spices.

1 Use the whole spice as is. One exception is whole coriander, which is rarely used as is because of its sharp flavor. But when it's rubbed into pork tenderloin or beef, for example, and then roasted, the spice's flavor transforms into a more mellow, slightly citrus one.

2 Grind the whole spice in a mortar and pestle or spice grinder. A coffee grinder reserved for spices works well. Grind until the texture looks like that of ground black pepper.

3 Dry-roast or toast the whole spice in a skillet for a few seconds or until the spice is one shade darker. Place the spice in a dry, heavy-bottom or nonstick skillet over medium-high heat. Shake the pan occasionally or stir the spices with a spoon about 1 minute or until the seeds turn reddish brown and become highly fragrant.

4 Dry-roast or toast the whole spice in a skillet for a few seconds or until the spice is one shade darker. Cool the spice; grind it in a mortar and pestle or spice grinder. A coffee grinder makes an excellent spice grinder, but reserve it for grinding spices only.

5 Stir-fry the whole spice in hot oil 10 to 20 seconds or until the spice is one shade darker and nutty smelling. Watch it carefully — it can burn in a matter of seconds.

6 Stir-fry the whole spice in hot oil 10 to 20 seconds or until the spice is one shade darker and nutty smelling. Remove it from the oil; grind it in a mortar and pestle or spice grinder. Allow the spice to cool before grinding it.

Coriander-Crusted Halibut with Mustard-Spinach Sauce

Coriander-Crusted Halibut with Mustard-Spinach Sauce

Freshly ground coriander adds a subtle citrus note to the spice dusting that coats the fish. Its flavor is an ideal match for the tangy mustard greens that make up the sauce. Chiles lend a bit of heat.

1½ tablespoons coriander seeds, ground
3 medium garlic cloves, finely chopped
1¼ teaspoons salt, divided
4 (6-oz.) boneless skinless halibut or mahimahi fillets
1 small onion, coarsely chopped
2 to 4 Thai, cayenne or serrano chiles
2 tablespoons vegetable oil, divided
1 teaspoon cumin seeds
1 cup tightly packed coarsely chopped mustard greens
1 cup tightly packed coarsely chopped fresh spinach
3 tablespoons fresh lime juice

1 In small bowl, combine ground coriander seeds, garlic and ¾ teaspoon of the salt; rub fish with spice mixture. Cover and refrigerate 1 to 2 hours.

2 Place onion and chiles in food processor; process until minced.

3 Heat 1 tablespoon of the oil in medium saucepan over medium heat. Add cumin seeds; cook 10 to 15 seconds or until fragrant. Add onion mixture; cook 2 to 4 minutes or until golden brown. Stir in mustard greens and spinach; cook 2 to 3 minutes or until greens are wilted, stirring occasionally. Transfer to food processor; add lime juice and remaining ½ teaspoon salt. Pulse until pureed.

4 Heat remaining 1 tablespoon oil in large skillet over medium heat. Add fish; cook 2 minutes, turning once.

Reduce heat to low; cover skillet. Cook an additional 3 to 4 minutes or until fish just begins to flake.

5 Spoon sauce onto serving platter; place fish on sauce. Serve immediately.

WINE/BEER You'll want a wine with good acidity and a touch of balanced sweetness to handle the heat and spice of these flavors. Try a top Vouvray, such as S.A. Huët Clos du Bourg Demi-Sec. A mellow beer would also play off the flavors nicely; we suggest the creamy, hoppy dark Anchor Porter.

4 servings

PER SERVING: 250 calories, 9.5 g total fat (1.5 g saturated fat), 34 g protein, 7.5 g carbohydrate, 90 mg cholesterol, 890 mg sodium, 2 g fiber

Raghavan Iyer, a native of India, is the author of Betty Crocker's *Indian Home Cooking* (Hungry Minds) and *The Turmeric Trail: Recipes and Memories from an Indian Childhood* (St. Martin's Press).

Roast Turkey with Rosemary-Garlic Crust

The Bird, The Sides, The Pie

Traditional Thanksgiving with a twist.

Text and Recipes by Maria Lorraine Binchet

Thanksgiving tables usually overflow with traditional dishes family and friends love and have come to expect. Yet even traditional foods benefit occasionally from a freshening up, a twist or a tweak to make them come alive and remain interesting.

This holiday menu features brightly flavored dishes that are new — yet familiar. Rather than breaking with tradition, we've chosen instead to update it. The centerpiece is a roast turkey covered with caramelized garlic and rosemary. Accompanying it are a savory bacon-cornbread stuffing and a sweet-tart pear chutney that serves as an alternate or an addition to the usual cranberry sauce. Whipped butternut squash with a crisp brown sugar crust steps in for the usual sweet potatoes, and a plump pumpkin pie with a gingery zing caps the meal.

Roast Turkey with Rosemary-Garlic Crust

The generous amounts of rosemary and garlic in this roast turkey mellow over the long cooking time. Thoroughly coating the turkey with butter helps keep it moist and aids in browning.

GARLIC-HERB BUTTER
- 1 cup unsalted butter, cut up
- 1 large garlic bulb, cloves thinly sliced
- ¾ cup coarsely chopped fresh rosemary
- 1 teaspoon salt

TURKEY
- 1 (12-lb.) turkey
- 1 tablespoon salt
- 1 tablespoon freshly ground pepper
- 3 carrots
- 3 ribs celery
- 1½ cups reduced-sodium chicken broth

1 Melt butter in medium skillet over low heat. Stir in garlic and rosemary; simmer 20 to 30 minutes or until garlic is soft and pale brown, stirring occasionally. Stir in 1 teaspoon salt. Place in medium bowl. Freeze 30 to 45 minutes or until slightly firm, stirring frequently. Or cover and refrigerate overnight.

2 Heat oven to 425°F. Sprinkle turkey inside and out with 1 tablespoon salt and pepper. Spread garlic-herb butter on outside of turkey, including crevices between thighs and wings. Place carrots and celery in bottom of roasting pan to form roasting rack; place turkey on vegetables. Pour broth into roasting pan.

3 Roast 30 minutes. Reduce oven temperature to 325°F.; roast an additional 1½ hours or until internal temperature reaches 180°F. to 185°F., basting with accumulated juices every 30 minutes. Remove from oven; cover loosely with foil. Let stand 20 minutes.

10 servings

PER SERVING: 495 calories, 29.5 g total fat (11.5 g saturated fat), 49 g protein, 6.5 g carbohydrate, 170 mg cholesterol, 980 mg sodium, 1.5 g fiber

Pear Chutney

This sweet-tart chutney works well as an addition to or a substitute for traditional cranberry sauce. For best flavor, make it at least one day before serving.

- 4 cups chopped (½ inch) peeled Anjou pears (about 4 pears)
- 1¼ cups diced onion
- 1 cup chopped pitted dried plums (prunes)
- ⅔ cup sugar
- ¾ cup cider vinegar
- ¼ cup lemon juice
- 2 tablespoons grated fresh ginger
- 2 teaspoons ground cinnamon
- 2 teaspoons grated lemon peel
- 1 teaspoon ground allspice
- ¼ teaspoon ground cloves
- ¼ teaspoon crushed red pepper

1 Place all ingredients in heavy large saucepan or nonreactive Dutch oven. Bring to a boil over medium-high heat. Reduce heat to medium-low to low; simmer 35 to 45 minutes or until slightly thickened. Cool to room temperature. (Chutney can be made up to 4 days ahead. Cover and refrigerate. Bring to room temperature before serving.)

4 cups

PER ¼ CUP: 75 calories, 0 g total fat (0 g saturated fat), .5 g protein, 19 g carbohydrate, 0 mg cholesterol, 0 mg sodium, 2 g fiber

Butternut Squash Brûlée

Butternut Squash Brûlée

This scrumptious dish's crowning touch is a crunchy, sugary crème brûlée-style top. Choose a brown sugar made from sugar cane. Brown sugar made from sugar beets has a tendency to burn when broiled. (Look for a brand such as C&H that's labeled "pure cane sugar.")

4 lb. (3 to 4) butternut squash, peeled, cubed (½ inch)

2 lb. (4 medium) russet potatoes, peeled, cubed (½ inch)
½ cup butter, cut up, softened
1 tablespoon salt
½ teaspoon grated lime peel
1 tablespoon adobo sauce or smoked paprika, or hot pepper sauce to taste*
⅔ cup packed brown cane sugar

1 Place squash and potatoes in large pot or Dutch oven; cover with cold water. Bring to a boil over medium-high heat. Reduce heat to medium-low; simmer 10 to 15 minutes or until soft. Drain; return to pan and cook over medium heat 1 minute, stirring, to remove excess water. Add butter, salt, lime peel and adobo sauce; beat at medium speed until blended and fluffy. Place in greased 13x9-inch baking pan or gratin dish. (Squash can be made to this point up to 1 day ahead. To reheat, bake at 350°F. 30 to 40 minutes or until heated through.)

2 Right before serving, heat broiler.

Evenly sift brown sugar over squash mixture. Broil 4 to 6 inches from heat 5 minutes or until sugar bubbles and darkens slightly.** (Make sure sugar does not burn.) Cool 5 to 10 minutes or until sugar hardens. Serve immediately.

TIPS *Adobo sauce is a dark red piquant Mexican sauce made from chiles, herbs and vinegar. Chipotle chiles are often canned in adobo sauce. For this recipe, purchase canned chipotle chiles and use the adobo sauce from the can.

**You also may use a small blowtorch to caramelize the sugar.

10 servings

PER SERVING: 295 calories, 9.5 g total fat (6 g saturated fat), 3 g protein, 53 g carbohydrate, 25 mg cholesterol, 810 mg sodium, 6.5 g fiber

Bacon-Cornbread Stuffing

Cornbread stuffing, a Thanksgiving tradition in many homes, gets a savory boost from bacon and sage. Red bell pepper adds a touch of sweetness and color. Creamed corn keeps the stuffing moist.

CORNBREAD
- 1 lb. bacon, cut into ½-inch pieces
- 1⅔ cups yellow cornmeal
- ⅔ cup all-purpose flour
- 3 tablespoons sugar
- 2 teaspoons baking powder
- ¼ teaspoon freshly ground pepper
- 1 cup buttermilk
- 2 eggs

STUFFING
- 2 cups diced onion
- 1½ cups diced celery
- 1 cup diced red bell pepper
- 1 (15-oz.) can creamed corn
- 3 eggs, beaten
- ¼ cup coarsely chopped fresh sage
- ½ teaspoon freshly ground pepper

1 Heat oven to 400°F. Place bacon in large skillet; cook over medium to medium-high heat 8 to 10 minutes or until crispy. Remove from pan; drain on paper towels. Reserve bacon drippings for cornbread and stuffing.

2 In large bowl, stir together cornmeal, flour, sugar, baking powder and ¼ teaspoon pepper. Add buttermilk, 2 eggs, bacon and 2 tablespoons of the reserved bacon drippings; stir just until combined. Brush 13x9-inch baking pan with 1 tablespoon of the reserved bacon drippings. Pour batter into pan.

3 Bake 15 to 20 minutes or until edges are lightly browned and toothpick inserted in center comes out clean. Cool completely in pan on wire rack. (Cornbread can be made up to 2 days ahead. Cover; store in refrigerator.) Break cornbread into small pieces; place in large bowl.

4 Heat 3 tablespoons of the reserved bacon drippings in large skillet over medium heat until hot. Add onion; cook 5 to 8 minutes or until tender and golden. Add celery and bell pepper; cook 5 to 8 minutes or until softened, stirring occasionally.

5 Add creamed corn and 3 eggs to cornbread; stir to combine. Add cooked vegetables, sage and ½ teaspoon pepper; stir until combined. (Stuffing can be made to this point up to 4 hours ahead. Cover and refrigerate. Increase baking time 10 to 15 minutes.)

6 Heat oven to 325°F. Brush 13x9-inch glass baking dish with 1 tablespoon of the reserved bacon drippings or melted butter. Place stuffing in baking dish; cover with foil. Bake 45 to 55 minutes or until heated through.

10 servings

PER SERVING: 375 calories, 18 g total fat (6.5 g saturated fat), 12.5 g protein, 41.5 g carbohydrate, 125 mg cholesterol, 510 mg sodium, 4 g fiber

Wines for the Thanksgiving Meal

Choosing wine for Thanksgiving may seem challenging, but it needn't be. Let the food take center stage and choose wines that won't compete with the dishes — full-bodied fruity or spicy white wines and lighter red wines usually work best. Here are a few suggestions:

Beaujolais Fruity, refreshing Beaujolais is possibly the best of all wines to accompany Thanksgiving. Look for Beaujolais from respected producers, such as those from Georges Duboeuf or Louis Jadot.

Chardonnay Look for clean, fruity Chardonnays, such as Chateau Souverain, Franciscan or Davis Bynum. Steer clear of those that are over-oaked or too buttery. Or try an original Chardonnay, a French white Burgundy such as Domaine Laroche, Chablis "Saint Martin" or the Joseph Drouhin Rully.

Riesling and Gewürztraminer The best of these lively, spicy white wines come from Alsace. Trimbach and Hugel are two good producers.

Viognier Once you try Viognier, with its tropical fruit and spice flavors, it may replace Chardonnay as your favorite white wine. Try Geyser Peak or Eberle, or the excellent Iron Horse.

Dessert Wines and Tawny Port The deep apricot and nut flavors found in late-harvest Gewürztraminers and Rieslings pair deliciously with pumpkin pie and other Thanksgiving desserts. Another excellent, surprising choice is 10- to 20-year-old tawny port. Savor the luscious caramel and deep, roasted nut flavors of Ramos-Pinto, Rozès, Barros or Poças.

Pumpkin-Ginger Pie with Ginger Cream

Pumpkin-Ginger Pie with Ginger Cream

The flavors of this pie are deeper than most pumpkin pies. For contrast, fresh ginger provides a bright, lively zing.

CRUST
- 1¼ cups all-purpose flour
- 1 tablespoon sugar
- ⅛ teaspoon salt
- 7 tablespoons unsalted butter, chilled, cut up
- 2 teaspoons grated fresh ginger
- 2 to 3 tablespoons water

FILLING
- 1 (15-oz.) can pure pumpkin
- 1 cup whipping cream
- 1 cup packed light brown sugar
- 3 eggs
- 1½ tablespoons grated fresh ginger
- 1½ teaspoons ground cinnamon
- ½ teaspoon ground allspice
- ½ teaspoon ground cloves
- ½ teaspoon salt

CREAM AND GARNISH
- 1½ cups whipping cream
- 1 tablespoon sugar
- ⅛ teaspoon ground ginger
- ⅓ cup minced crystallized ginger

1 In medium bowl, stir together flour, 1 tablespoon sugar and salt. Add butter and 2 teaspoons fresh ginger. With pastry blender or 2 knives, cut butter into flour mixture until mixture resembles coarse crumbs with some pea-sized pieces. Add 2 tablespoons of the water; stir with fork until dough forms, adding additional water if necessary. Shape into flat round; cover and refrigerate 30 minutes.

2 Heat oven to 375°F. Roll dough into 12-inch round. Place in 9-inch pie plate; flute edges. Refrigerate.

3 In medium bowl, whisk together all filling ingredients until well blended; pour into crust.

4 Bake 10 minutes; loosely cover crust with foil. Bake an additional 30 to 35 minutes or until outside edges are set (center of pie will shake slightly when tapped but will set during cooling). Cool completely on wire rack.

5 In medium bowl, beat 1½ cups cream, 1 tablespoon sugar and ⅛ teaspoon ginger at medium-high speed 1 to 3 minutes or until soft peaks form. Serve pie with whipped cream; sprinkle with crystallized ginger.

8 servings

PER SERVING: 570 calories, 35.5 g total fat (21.5 g saturated fat), 7 g protein, 58.5 g carbohydrate, 190 mg cholesterol, 265 mg sodium, 2.5 g fiber

Maria Lorraine Binchet writes about food and wine from Napa Valley, California.

Salmon Ravioli

Ravioli

It's fun to make, even better to eat.

Text and Recipes by G. Franco Romagnoli

Ravioli is part of the much-loved Italian family of filled pastas. Practically every Italian town has its own version: agnolotti, anolini, cappelletti, tortelli and tortellini, ravioli and ravioloni. Spoken out loud, they might well be the lyrics of a zesty Italian opera.

If you've never made ravioli, you're in for a surprise: It's easier to make than it appears. Food processors and pasta machines simplify the job. And these recipes make large ravioli, traditionally called ravioloni, speeding up the process. This is a dish that's comfortably within the reach of home cooks. Making it is almost as rewarding as eating it.

Salmon Ravioli

The full taste of wild Atlantic salmon is perfect for these ravioli and appropriate for an elegant spring meal. Serve with either Butter and Sage White Sauce *(page 78) or* Tomato, Butter and Basil Sauce *(page 81).*

1 (1-lb.) salmon fillet
¼ cup capers, drained, rinsed
2 tablespoons minced fresh Italian parsley
1 tablespoon unseasoned dry bread crumbs
1 teaspoon salt
¼ teaspoon freshly ground pepper
3 tablespoons lemon juice
1 tablespoon extra-virgin olive oil
1 egg yolk
1 recipe *Ravioli Dough* (pg. 80)

1 Poach salmon in medium skillet in lightly salted gently boiling water 1 to 2 minutes or until outer edges are opaque but center is rare (do not overcook). Drain well on paper towels; cool. Remove skin and bones; flake or cut into small pieces. Place in medium bowl.
2 Add all remaining ingredients except dough; stir with fork until blended. If mixture is soft and doesn't hold together, add an additional 1 to 2 tablespoons bread crumbs. Cover and refrigerate 30 minutes.

3 Divide dough into 3 pieces. Working with 1 piece of dough at a time (keep remaining dough covered), flatten dough to about ¼ inch with heel of hand.
4 Set pasta machine at widest opening. Roll dough through; fold in half lengthwise; press gently. Continue rolling and folding dough 4 more times. Dough should be smooth with a silky texture, and width of dough should be about same width as opening of pasta machine.
5 Set pasta machine to next narrowest setting. Roll dough through twice, but do not fold in half. Repeat, reducing size of opening after rolling dough through each setting twice. Dough will continue to get thinner and longer (you may need to drape it over your arm as you feed it into the machine and gently pull it out as it drapes onto the base). If you find the length difficult to handle, cut dough in half and work with smaller pieces.
6 Continue rolling until dough is thin but not paper-thin. You may not need to roll it on the most narrow setting (we went up to setting number 6 out of 7 on the Atlas pasta machine).
7 Cut pasta sheets in 2 equal lengths; place on lightly floured surface. Cover with plastic wrap (it is important dough does not dry out). Repeat with remaining dough.
8 Working with 1 strip at a time, cut dough crosswise into 3½-inch pieces.

Place slightly heaping 1 tablespoon filling on bottom half of each piece. With pastry brush dipped in water, moisten pasta around filling to edges. Fold top half of pasta over filling; gently press with fingertips to eliminate air bubbles and seal pasta. Trim cut edges with fluted pastry wheel, if desired. Place on towel-lined baking sheet; cover with plastic wrap. (Ravioli can be made up to 3 weeks ahead and frozen. Place shaped ravioli on towel-lined pan in freezer up to 4 hours or until ravioli are frozen. Once frozen, place ravioli in large resealable plastic bag or airtight container.)
9 Bring large pot of salted water to a boil. Cook fresh or frozen ravioli 12 to 15 minutes (begin timing once water returns to a boil) or until tender and ravioli float to surface. Remove with slotted spoon.
WINE The combination of salmon and basil calls for a dry, slightly herbal white wine. Either Geyser Peak Sauvignon Blanc from California or Feudi di San Gregorio Greco di Tufo from Italy works nicely here.
4 (6-ravioli) servings

PER SERVING: 540 calories, 18 g total fat (4 g saturated fat), 33.5 g protein, 57.5 g carbohydrate, 280 mg cholesterol, 1235 mg sodium, 2.5 g fiber

Spinach Ravioli with Fresh Mint and
Tomato, Butter and Basil Sauce

Butter and Sage White Sauce

*This sauce's strength rests with its
delicate taste and, above all, with its
aroma. If you wish, it may be sprinkled
with thin strips of prosciutto, either at
the end of cooking or as a tasty frill on
top of the ravioli when served.*

12 tablespoons unsalted
    butter, divided
1 cup loosely packed fresh
    sage, coarsely chopped
    (10 tablespoons)
3 tablespoons all-purpose flour
1 cup half-and-half
1 cup milk
1 teaspoon white pepper
½ teaspoon salt

1 cup thinly sliced prosciutto,
    cut into ¼-inch strips,
    if desired*

1 Melt 6 tablespoons of the butter in
large skillet over medium heat. Stir in
sage; cook just until limp. Whisk in
flour; cook 1 minute. Add half-and-
half and milk; stir until mixture is
smooth. Bring to a boil.

Spinach Ravioli with Fresh Mint

The classic à la Florentine combination of spinach and cheese acquires a new zest here with the addition of fresh mint. Serve with either Butter and Sage White Sauce *(page 78) or* Tomato, Butter and Basil Sauce *(page 81).*

- 1 (10-oz.) pkg. frozen chopped spinach, thawed
- 1 (8-oz.) container ricotta cheese
- ¼ cup (1 oz.) freshly grated Parmigiano-Reggiano cheese
- ¼ cup chopped fresh mint
- 1 egg
- 1 tablespoon unseasoned dry bread crumbs
- ½ teaspoon salt
- ½ teaspoon white pepper
- ¼ teaspoon freshly grated nutmeg
- 1 recipe *Ravioli Dough* (pg. 80)

1 Squeeze spinach until as dry as possible. Put spinach and all remaining ingredients except dough in large bowl. Stir with fork until blended. If mixture is soft and doesn't hold together, add an additional 1 to 2 tablespoons bread crumbs. Cover and refrigerate 30 minutes.

2 Divide dough into 3 pieces. Working with 1 piece of dough at a time (keep remaining dough covered), flatten dough to about ¼ inch with heel of hand.

3 Set pasta machine at widest opening. Roll dough through; fold in half lengthwise; press gently. Continue rolling and folding dough 4 more times. Dough should be smooth with a silky texture, and width of dough should be about same width as opening of pasta machine.

4 Set pasta machine to next narrowest setting. Roll dough through twice, but do not fold in half. Repeat, reducing size of opening after rolling

dough through each setting twice. Dough will continue to get thinner and longer (you may need to drape it over your arm as you feed it into the machine and gently pull it out as it drapes onto the base). If you find the length difficult to handle, cut dough in half and work with smaller pieces.

5 Continue rolling until dough is thin but not paper-thin. You may not need to roll it on the most narrow setting (we went up to setting number 6 out of 7 on the Atlas pasta machine).

6 Cut pasta sheets in 2 equal lengths; place on lightly floured surface. Cover with plastic wrap (it is important dough does not dry out). Repeat with remaining dough.

7 Working with 1 strip at a time, cut dough crosswise into 3½-inch pieces. Place scant 1 tablespoon filling on bottom half of each piece. With pastry brush dipped in water, moisten pasta around filling to edges. Fold top half of pasta over filling; gently press with fingertips to eliminate air bubbles and seal pasta. Trim cut edges with fluted pastry wheel, if desired. Place on towel-lined baking sheet; cover with plastic wrap. (Ravioli can be made up to 3 weeks ahead and frozen. Place shaped ravioli on towel-lined pan in freezer up to 4 hours or until ravioli are frozen. Once frozen, place ravioli in large resealable plastic bag or airtight container.)

8 Bring large pot of salted water to a boil. Cook fresh or frozen ravioli 12 to 15 minutes (begin timing once water returns to a boil) or until tender and ravioli float to surface. Remove with slotted spoon.

WINE A rich Italian red pairs well with the cheese in this dish. Try either Michele Chiarlo Barbera d'Asti or Zenato "Ripasso" Valpolicella.

4 (6-ravioli) servings

PER SERVING: 495 calories, 16 g total fat (6 g saturated fat), 24.5 g protein, 62.5 g carbohydrate, 235 mg cholesterol, 900 mg sodium, 3.5 g fiber

2 Add remaining 6 tablespoons butter, pepper and salt. Boil 1 minute. Stir in prosciutto.

TIP *Prosciutto is an Italian-style, salt-cured, unsmoked ham.

4 servings

PER SERVING: 500 calories, 47 g total fat (28 g saturated fat), 10.5 g protein, 11 g carbohydrate, 135 mg cholesterol, 610 mg sodium, .5 g fiber

Ravioli Dough

Gone are the days of large pastry boards and yard-long rolling pins. The food processor does the mixing and first kneading of the dough; the pasta machine completes the kneading and does the rolling.

3 cups all-purpose flour
½ teaspoon salt
4 eggs, room temperature*
1 tablespoon olive oil

1 Place flour and salt in food processor; pulse until blended. In medium bowl, whisk together eggs and oil until combined. With motor running, pour egg mixture through feed tube into food processor. Pulse 30 seconds or until mixture is combined. (Be careful not to overmix; dough should not form ball.) Mixture should cling together when pinched. (If too dry, add 1 to 2 teaspoons water; if too wet, add 1 to 2 teaspoons flour.)

2 Turn out dough onto surface; press together to form ball. Knead a couple of times until smooth. Cover with plastic wrap; let stand at room temperature 20 minutes.

TIP *To warm eggs quickly, place whole eggs in bowl of hot water. Let stand 5 to 10 minutes.

PER ¼ RECIPE: 445 calories, 9.5 g total fat (2 g saturated fat), 16 g protein, 72 g carbohydrate, 215 mg cholesterol, 355 mg sodium, 2.5 g fiber

1 To make the pasta, mix the ingredients in a food processor just until they are combined. The dough should cling together when pinched.

2 Set the pasta machine rollers at their widest setting. Divide the dough into thirds. Shape one section into a rectangle and feed it through the rollers.

3 After the dough goes through the rollers, fold it in half lengthwise and gently press the ends together. Repeat rolling and folding four more times at this setting.

4 Reduce the opening of the rollers one setting; roll the dough through twice but don't fold it in half. Repeat until the dough is thin and the width of the rollers.

5 To assemble the ravioli, place the filling on one half of a strip of dough. Fold the other half over the filling. Gently press the dough to seal the pasta and eliminate air bubbles.

6 To make the ravioli more attractive, trim the edges with a fluted pastry wheel or a knife. To keep ravioli from drying out, place on a towel-lined baking sheet and cover with plastic.

Tomato, Butter and Basil Sauce

This simple tomato sauce can accompany all sorts of pasta, and, warm or cold, it's also a good sauce for meat and fish dishes. It can be streamlined even further by eliminating the cream.

- 2 cups canned plum tomatoes, undrained
- ½ cup coarsely chopped fresh basil
- 6 tablespoons unsalted butter
- ½ teaspoon salt
- ½ teaspoon sugar
- ½ cup whipping cream

1 Pass tomatoes through food mill or sieve, collecting pulp and juice in large skillet. Add basil; bring to a boil over medium-high heat. Reduce heat to low. Add butter, salt and sugar. Simmer 10 to 12 minutes, stirring constantly.

2 Just before serving, stir in cream.

TIP Start this sauce when the ravioli are put in boiling water; it will be ready by the time they are cooked.

4 servings

PER SERVING: 265 calories, 27 g total fat (16.5 g saturated fat), 2 g protein, 7 g carbohydrate, 80 mg cholesterol, 500 mg sodium, 1.5 g fiber

Gorgonzola-Fig Ravioli

Blending the sharp, salty taste of Gorgonzola cheese with the sweetness of fruit — accompanied by a sip or two of a robust red wine — is a common way of closing an Italian meal. These ravioli open a meal, but a glass of hearty red wine goes nicely here, too. Serve with Butter and Sage White Sauce (page 78).

- ¾ cup (4 oz.) dried white or dark figs
- 2 cups (8 oz.) crumbled Gorgonzola cheese
- 1 cup (4 oz.) freshly grated Parmesan cheese
- 1 tablespoon unseasoned dry bread crumbs
- 1 egg yolk
- 1 recipe *Ravioli Dough* (page 80)

1 Place figs in medium bowl; cover with boiling water. Let stand 3 to 4 minutes to soften. Drain; finely chop.

2 In large bowl, combine figs and all remaining ingredients except dough; stir with fork until blended. If mixture is soft and doesn't hold together, add an additional 1 to 2 tablespoons bread crumbs. Cover and refrigerate 30 minutes.

3 Divide dough into 3 pieces. Working with 1 piece of dough at a time (keep remaining dough covered), flatten dough to about ¼ inch with heel of hand.

4 Set pasta machine at widest opening. Roll dough through; fold in half lengthwise; press gently. Continue rolling and folding dough 4 more times. Dough should be smooth with a silky texture, and width of dough should be about same width as opening of pasta machine.

5 Set pasta machine to next narrowest setting. Roll dough through twice, but do not fold in half. Repeat, reducing size of opening after rolling dough through each setting twice. Dough will continue to get thinner and longer (you may need to drape it over your arm as you feed it into the machine and gently pull it out as it drapes onto the base). If you find the length difficult to handle, cut dough in half and work with smaller pieces.

6 Continue rolling until dough is thin but not paper-thin. You may not need to roll it on the most narrow setting (we went up to setting number 6 out of 7 on the Atlas pasta machine).

7 Cut pasta sheets in 2 equal lengths; place on lightly floured surface. Cover with plastic wrap (it is important dough does not dry out). Repeat with remaining dough.

8 Working with 1 strip at a time, cut dough crosswise into 3½-inch pieces. Place 1 tablespoon filling on bottom half of each piece. With pastry brush dipped in water, moisten pasta around filling to edges. Fold top half of pasta over filling; gently press with fingertips to eliminate air bubbles and seal pasta. Trim cut edges with fluted pastry wheel, if desired. Place on towel-lined baking sheet; cover with plastic wrap. (Ravioli can be made up to 3 weeks ahead and frozen. Place shaped ravioli on towel-lined pan in freezer up to 4 hours or until ravioli are frozen. Once frozen, place ravioli in large resealable plastic bag or airtight container.)

9 Bring large pot of salted water to a boil. Cook fresh or frozen ravioli 12 to 15 minutes (begin timing once water returns to a boil) or until tender and ravioli float to surface. Remove with slotted spoon.

WINE Gorgonzola needs a very strong red to stand up to its intensity. A good value is Badia a Coltibuono "Cetamura" Chianti. For a fuller-flavored red, Bruno Giacosa Nebbiolo d'Alba is exquisite.

4 (6-ravioli) servings

PER SERVING: 715 calories, 30 g total fat (15.5 g saturated fat), 35.5 g protein, 76 g carbohydrate, 275 mg cholesterol, 1310 mg sodium, 4.5 g fiber

G. Franco Romagnoli, a native of Rome, is a Boston-based cooking instructor and writer specializing in Italian foods. He is the author of *A Thousand Bells at Noon.*

Greek Grilled Shrimp

Shrimp on a Stick

Simple ideas, sophisticated tastes.

Text and Recipes by Bruce Weinstein and Mark Scarbrough

Fast. Easy. Flavorful. The requirements for a summertime dinner are that simple. You don't want to spend an hour at the stove, but you're not willing to sacrifice big, bold tastes for convenience. What's one solution? Light the coals and bring on the shrimp.

Shrimp cooks in minutes, requires minimal preparation and is the perfect foil for a wide range of seasonings, from sweet to spicy. Steeping it in marinades ensures deep flavors. Skewering it makes a fun presentation. And cooking shrimp on the grill adds the smoky notes that define warm-weather cooking.

Greek Grilled Shrimp

Inspired by the flavors of the Greek isles, these shrimp skewers are elegant enough for a sit-down dinner party but easy enough for a Saturday picnic. Orange sections and almond biscotti make a great dessert.

- ⅓ cup extra-virgin olive oil
- 2 garlic cloves, minced
- 2 tablespoons capers, drained, coarsely chopped
- 2 tablespoons chopped fresh dill
- 1 tablespoon chopped fresh oregano
- 2 teaspoons finely grated lemon peel
- 2 teaspoons fennel seeds, crushed*
- 1 teaspoon salt
- ½ teaspoon freshly ground pepper
- 1½ lb. shelled, deveined uncooked large shrimp (16 to 20 per pound)
- 1 (14-oz.) can artichoke hearts, drained, halved
- 8 cherry tomatoes
- 1 cup (4 oz.) crumbled feta cheese

1 In large bowl, stir together oil, garlic, capers, dill, oregano, lemon peel, fennel seeds, salt and pepper. Stir in shrimp to coat; cover and refrigerate at least 2 hours or up to 4 hours.
2 Heat grill. Equally divide and thread shrimp, artichoke hearts and tomatoes onto 4 (10- to 12-inch) metal skewers. Brush marinade over shrimp. Place on gas grill over medium heat or on charcoal grill 4 to 6 inches from medium coals. Cook 3 minutes; turn. Place feta on shrimp. Cook an additional 3 minutes or until shrimp turn pink and cheese is melted.
TIP *Crush fennel seeds with mortar and pestle, flat side of meat mallet or bottom of saucepan.
WINE Choose a spicy white wine to complement the shrimp's seasonings, such as Côtes du Rhône Blanc from E. Guigal, or an Oregon Pinot Gris, such as Rex Hill.

4 servings

PER SERVING: 345 calories, 18.5 g total fat (7 g saturated fat), 34 g protein, 11.5 g carbohydrate, 275 mg cholesterol, 1245 mg sodium, 4 g fiber

Citrus-Marinated Shrimp

Citrus fruit and mint provide the flavoring for a very summery marinade that takes just minutes to make. Light and simple, these zesty grilled shrimp are great fare for family barbecues or weekend get-togethers. Serve the shrimp alongside rice or orzo or with a vinegared salad of green beans and almonds.

- ¼ cup extra-virgin olive oil
- 1 tablespoon grated grapefruit peel
- 1 tablespoon grated lemon peel
- 1 tablespoon grated tangerine peel
- 1 teaspoon chopped fresh mint
- ½ teaspoon salt
- 1½ lb. shelled, deveined uncooked large shrimp (16 to 20 per pound)

1 In medium bowl, stir together all ingredients except shrimp. Stir in shrimp to coat; cover and refrigerate at least 2 hours or overnight.
2 Heat grill. Remove shrimp from marinade, keeping them coated with citrus peel and mint; discard remaining marinade. Thread shrimp onto 4 (10- to 12-inch) metal skewers. Place on gas grill over medium heat or on charcoal grill 4 to 6 inches from medium coals. Cook 5 to 6 minutes or until shrimp turn pink, turning once. Serve hot or at room temperature.
WINE The citrus notes of this dish need a similarly flavored dry white wine. Lindemans "Bin 95" Sauvignon Blanc pairs well, as does the rich and elegant Flora Springs "Soliloquy" Sauvignon Blanc from Napa.

4 servings

PER SERVING: 155 calories, 4.5 g total fat (1 g saturated fat), 26 g protein, .5 g carbohydrate, 240 mg cholesterol, 350 mg sodium, 0 g fiber

Mole-Rubbed Shrimp

Mole-Rubbed Shrimp

This rub is an adaptation of mole, a Mexican sauce made with chiles and unsweetened chocolate. If you can't find New Mexican red chiles, substitute 1½ tablespoons chili powder and omit the ground cumin. Accompany this fiery dish with a fresh tomato salsa.

1 New Mexican dried red chile, veins and seeds removed
1½ teaspoons unsweetened cocoa
1 teaspoon ground cumin
¾ teaspoon salt, divided
¼ teaspoon cinnamon
2 tablespoons sliced almonds, toasted*
2 tablespoons coarsely chopped pepitas (green pumpkin seeds), toasted*
1½ lb. shelled, deveined uncooked large shrimp (16 to 20 per pound)
2 tablespoons plus 2 teaspoons vegetable oil, divided
1 large ripe plantain, peeled, cut crosswise into 12 pieces**

1 In spice grinder or clean coffee grinder, grind chile until finely powdered. Add cocoa, cumin, ½ teaspoon of the salt and cinnamon; grind until well combined. Add toasted almonds and pepitas; grind until powdered, making sure paste doesn't form.

2 In large bowl, toss shrimp with 2 tablespoons of the oil. Stir in spice mixture; toss to coat. Cover and let stand at room temperature 30 minutes.

3 In small bowl, combine remaining 2 teaspoons oil and ¼ teaspoon salt. Add plantain; toss to coat.

4 Heat grill. Alternately thread

shrimp and plantains horizontally onto 4 (10- to 12-inch) metal skewers. Place on gas grill over medium heat or on charcoal grill 4 to 6 inches from medium coals. Cook 5 to 6 minutes or until shrimp turn pink, turning once.

TIPS *To toast almonds and pepitas, place on baking sheet; bake at 350°F. for 5 minutes or until lightly browned.

**Plantains are a type of cooking banana. Skin color, not firmness, is an indicator of ripeness. Look for fruit that is yellow with some blackish-brown spots.

BEER/WINE A dark Mexican beer is perfect for this shrimp; Negra Modelo is about as good as it gets. For wine, look for a spicy red that is not too heavy; Coppola "Diamond Label" Syrah from California fits the bill.

4 servings

PER SERVING: 340 calories, 14 g total fat (2.5 g saturated fat), 29 g protein, 27 g carbohydrate, 240 mg cholesterol, 720 mg sodium, 3 g fiber

Shrimp in Beer Marinade

Belgian white beer is lightly scented with orange rind and spices, a good match for the shrimp. But you can substitute any beer. Marinating overnight infuses the flavors more deeply. You might want to serve the skewers with salty French fries and malt vinegar. This dish is easily doubled or tripled.

1 (12-oz.) bottle Belgian white beer or your favorite beer
1 tablespoon grated fresh ginger
2 teaspoons Dijon mustard
½ teaspoon freshly ground pepper
¼ teaspoon salt
1½ lb. shelled, deveined uncooked large shrimp (16 to 20 per pound)

1 In large bowl, whisk together all ingredients except shrimp. Stir in shrimp to coat. Cover and refrigerate at least 2 hours or overnight.
2 Heat grill. Thread shrimp onto

4 (10- to 12-inch) metal skewers. Place on gas grill over medium heat or on charcoal grill 4 to 6 inches from medium coals. Cook 5 minutes or until shrimp turn pink, brushing occasionally with marinade and turning once.

BEER/WINE This beer marinade calls for a flavorful beer; Chimay Première from Belgium is a good selection. Or try a sparkling wine, such as the dry nonvintage Mumm Napa Blanc de Noirs.

4 servings

PER SERVING: 105 calories, 1 g total fat (.5 g saturated fat), 17.5 g protein, 2 g carbohydrate, 160 mg cholesterol, 275 mg sodium, .5 g fiber

Hot Honey Shrimp Skewers

This piquant honey marinade becomes the barbecue baste once the shrimp go on the grill. Crushed red pepper provides a spicy kick, but you can adjust the amount to your taste. Serve nutty wild rice as a side dish.

½ cup wildflower honey*
2 tablespoons canola oil
3 tablespoons frozen cranberry juice concentrate, thawed
2 teaspoons crushed red pepper
½ teaspoon salt
Dash nutmeg
1½ lb. shelled, deveined uncooked large shrimp (16 to 20 per pound)
4 ears corn, husked, cut crosswise into 1-inch pieces
2 red bell peppers, cut into 1½-inch pieces

1 In small saucepan, melt honey with oil over low heat. Bring to a boil; remove from heat. Stir in cranberry juice concentrate, red pepper, salt and nutmeg. Let stand at room temperature 10 to 15 minutes or until cool.
2 Place shrimp in large bowl; pour honey marinade over shrimp, stirring to coat. Cover and refrigerate at least 2 hours or overnight.
3 Heat grill. Alternately thread shrimp, corn and bell peppers onto

Hot Honey Shrimp Skewers

8 (8- to 10-inch) metal skewers. (If corn is difficult to thread, use small knife to cut hole through corn first.) Place on gas grill over medium heat or on charcoal grill 4 to 6 inches from medium coals. Cook 8 to 10 minutes or until shrimp turn pink, turning once and basting occasionally with marinade.

TIP *Wildflower honeys are usually medium to dark in color and more robust in flavor. Any honey can be substituted in this recipe.

BEER/WINE Any number of pale ales pick up on this dish's honey flavors; Bass from England is a fine choice. For wine, try a lighter red, such as Alderbrook Pinot Noir from Sonoma.

4 servings

PER SERVING: 325 calories, 6 g total fat (1 g saturated fat), 29 g protein, 43 g carbohydrate, 240 mg cholesterol, 440 mg sodium, 3 g fiber

New York-based food writers Bruce Weinstein and Mark Scarbrough are the authors of *The Ultimate Shrimp Book* (William Morrow).

The Shrimp Market; How to Buy Shrimp

Strictly speaking, there's no such thing as fresh shrimp. With few exceptions, most shrimp sold in North America are frozen during harvest. This is done because fresh shrimp are highly perishable. Shrimp freeze well, and freezing preserves their flavor and allows producers to safely ship them.

Frozen or thawed You can buy shrimp either frozen or thawed. Make sure the thawed shrimp are "fresh" — the shrimp should be thawed just before being sold. If they've been handled properly, thawed shrimp should smell clean, like the ocean. If they smell like ammonia or rotten eggs, they've spoiled. While it's also legal to extend shelf-life by "doping" the shrimp with chlorine, this gives the shrimp a distinctive swimming pool-like aroma. It's not harmful, but it's not pleasant.

Check appearance Thawed shrimp meat should look translucent. There should be no black spots at the shells' joints, which are a sign of deterioration. And there shouldn't be yellowing at the neck, the thickest end. Dipping shrimp in a sodium bisulfite solution is a practice sometimes used to prevent black spots and to control decay. But too much of this chemical can result in a dusty yellow residue and a rough, sandpaper-like quality in the meat.

Size Shrimp are sold by size, which is indicated by the count (under 12, 12 to 16, 16 to 20, etc.). These loose terms represent the number of shrimp per pound. Unfortunately, there are no standards that must be followed regarding size, so you may find that medium shrimp at one retailer means 35 to 40 shrimp per pound while at another retailer, medium shrimp means 20 to 25 per pound.

For these recipes, we call for large shrimp, 16 to 20 per pound. If you can't find this size, buy the largest available. The larger the shrimp, the easier they are to peel, devein and skewer.

Peeling & Deveining

For all of the recipes here, the shrimp must be peeled before cooking. You also may devein them, which entails removing the black vein (the shrimp's digestive track) that runs down the back of the shrimp. (While most people find shrimp more appetizing if the vein is removed, this step is optional.) If you don't see the vein, it may be because your shrimp were farm-raised and "purged" before being sent to market, making the vein invisible and deveining unnecessary.

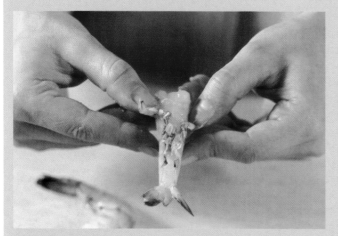

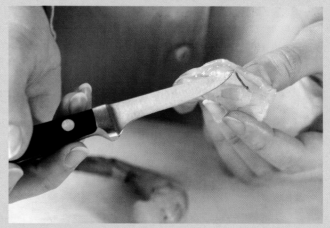

To peel Gently press your thumbs on the inside curve of the shrimp to pry the shell loose. Peel away the shell, leaving the final tail segment intact for a small "handle" and a prettier presentation.

To devein Use a paring knife, make a ¼-inch-deep slit along the back, stopping just before the tail. Holding the shrimp under cool, running water, open the meat, exposing the vein. Carefully pull out the vein with a knife.

Success Tips

Shrimp are so easy to prepare that there are only a few basic tips for success.

- If you buy thawed shrimp, use them the day you buy them.

- You may buy frozen shrimp for these recipes but be careful not to purchase frozen cooked shrimp. Instead, look for frozen raw shrimp.

  To thaw, place shrimp in a single layer in the refrigerator on a rimmed baking sheet; cover with plastic wrap. Thawing may take up to 24 hours. Keep the shrimp refrigerated until you're ready to use them.

- Toss the shrimp once or twice while they marinate, especially if the recipe has a long marinating time. However, never let them sit in citrus- or vinegar-based marinades longer than the recipe suggests because the meat will become tough.

- Don't use the marinade as a sauce unless it has been boiled for 10 minutes.

- You can use a broiler instead of a grill for these recipes. Heat the broiler, then lay the skewered shrimp on a broiler pan or baking sheet lined with foil. Place the pan 4 to 6 inches from the heat source. Turn the skewers once during cooking, according to the recipe.

- Watch cooking times carefully. It's easy to overcook shrimp, making them dry and rubbery. Shrimp should turn pink and be slightly firm but still have a little give to the meat. If they are totally firm, they are overcooked.

Skewer Options

Metal or wooden skewers can be used for shrimp, but for a more lively presentation — and some additional flavor — try using one of the following natural alternatives.

Rosemary Cut 10-inch-long stalks. Starting at the bottom of the stalk, remove all of the leaves up to 2 inches from the tip. Soak the stalks in water for 20 minutes before threading on the food. Rosemary works well with *Greek Grilled Shrimp* (page 83).

Lemon Grass

Lemon Grass Purchase firm stalks. To prepare them, discard the soft tops. Slit and peel off the outer leaves. Then soak the stalks in water for 20 minutes. Use lemon grass with *Hot Honey Shrimp Skewers* (page 85).

Cinnamon Sticks

Cinnamon Sticks To make cinnamon stick skewers, cut the sticks in half lengthwise. (Look for long sticks of cinnamon in specialty food stores.) Soak the sticks in water for 20 minutes. Pierce the shrimp with a paring knife to make a guide hole for the sticks. Pair cinnamon sticks with *Mole-Rubbed Shrimp* (page 84).

Sugar Cane

Sugar Cane To prepare sugar cane for skewers, slice canned or fresh peeled sugar cane, or packaged sugar cane swizzle sticks, into 7-inch sticks, $1/4$ inch in diameter. Soak the canes in water for 20 minutes. Then pierce the shrimp with a paring knife, making a small guide hole for inserting the cane. Use sugar canes with *Citrus-Marinated Shrimp* (page 83).

Fresh Spinach Chicken with Balsamic Glaze

A Splash of Balsamic

Just a little of this sweet-tart condiment livens up everyday dishes.

Text and Recipes by Jill Van Cleave

In Renaissance Italy, cooking with balsamic vinegar of Modena was unthinkable. Instead, this remarkable condiment was drunk as medicine and sipped as a liqueur by dignitaries and aristocrats. Aged balsamic vinegar was not even commercially available outside of Italy until the latter half of the 20th century.

Today, balsamic vinegar is one of Italy's most prized food exports, finding a place in home kitchens the world over. Many American supermarkets stock a variety of brands at varying prices. Most of them fall into a category called "commercial" balsamic vinegar and are used primarily for cooking and salad dressings. Cooks relish its tangy, caramel-like flavor with suggestions of dark raisins and sugary plums. More rare and far more expensive is "traditional" balsamic, which is too pricey to cook with and does not benefit from being heated. This thick, syrupy and intensely flavored balsamic is used as a condiment, most often drizzled sparingly over cooked foods, Parmesan cheese or fruit.

The commercial balsamics offer a variety of tastes and are priced to suit all budgets. Vinegars with pronounced acidity can be paired with olive oil in dressings and marinades or used to deglaze pan juices. When reduced over heat to a consistency of thickened syrup, balsamic becomes more flavorful; its berry characteristics are perfect for glazing cooked meats or vegetables. Balsamic also adds richness and sweet-sour complexity to foods when splashed onto salads or vegetables, stirred into sauces, used in braising meats or stews, or added to pasta or risotto.

Because balsamic is a versatile vinegar, it is capable of enhancing everyday meals. Used judiciously, this full-flavored condiment can turn ordinary dishes into extraordinary ones.

Fresh Spinach Chicken with Balsamic Glaze

This quick-cooking sauté is an ideal weekday meal; it's ready in three easy steps and uses only one skillet. The vinegar plus a touch of brown sugar are reduced with the pan juices at the last minute to create a deliciously simple sweet-sour glaze to drizzle on the plate.

- 4 boneless skinless chicken breast halves
- ¼ teaspoon plus ⅛ teaspoon salt, divided
- ¼ teaspoon freshly ground pepper
- 1 tablespoon olive oil
- 1 orange or red bell pepper, cut into thin strips
- 1 cup thinly sliced red onion
- 2 garlic cloves, minced
- 6 cups loosely packed fresh spinach
- ⅓ cup balsamic vinegar
- ½ teaspoon packed light brown sugar

1 Sprinkle both sides of chicken with ¼ teaspoon of the salt and pepper. Heat oil in large skillet over medium-high heat until hot. Add chicken; cook 4 to 6 minutes or until brown, turning once. Cover and reduce heat to medium; cook 4 minutes or until chicken is no longer pink in center and juices run clear. Place on plate; loosely cover to keep warm.

2 Increase heat to medium-high. To same skillet, add bell pepper, onion and garlic. Cook 1 to 2 minutes or until vegetables just begin to soften. Add spinach; sprinkle with remaining ⅛ teaspoon salt. Remove from heat; toss until spinach is barely wilted. Place on serving plates or platter. Top with chicken.

3 Return same skillet to high heat. Add vinegar and brown sugar. Bring to a boil; boil 30 to 60 seconds or until slightly thickened, scraping up browned bits from bottom of skillet. Drizzle balsamic glaze around chicken and vegetables.

WINE An Australian Shiraz is one of the best wines for this chicken. Rosemount "Diamond Label" is very flavorful, while Peter Lehmann Barossa has a bit more spice and body.

4 servings

PER SERVING: 215 calories, 7 g total fat (1.5 g saturated fat), 29 g protein, 9 g carbohydrate, 65 mg cholesterol, 345 mg sodium, 3 g fiber

Grilled Fennel Pork Tenderloin
with Balsamic Vegetables

Grilled Fennel Pork Tenderloin with Balsamic Vegetables

For this easy grilled dinner, pork tenderloins are marinated in a flavorful paste of fennel seeds and fresh orange spiked with balsamic vinegar. The paste enhances the flavor of the meat, and it eliminates the need to make a sauce. If desired, shave aged Parmesan cheese over the grilled vegetables before drizzling them with the vinegar.

MARINADE
- 8 medium garlic cloves, coarsely chopped
- 2 tablespoons fennel seeds, finely crushed*
- 2 tablespoons orange juice
- 1 tablespoon grated orange peel
- ¼ teaspoon freshly ground pepper
- ¼ teaspoon kosher (coarse) salt
- 2 tablespoons balsamic vinegar
- ¼ cup olive oil

PORK AND VEGETABLES
- 2 (¾- to 1-lb.) pork tenderloins
- 4 zucchini, cut diagonally into ¼-inch slices
- 2 fennel bulbs, fronds removed and discarded, cut vertically into ¼-inch slices
- 1 tablespoon olive oil
- ½ teaspoon kosher (coarse) salt
- ¼ teaspoon freshly ground pepper
- 2 tablespoons balsamic vinegar

1 In food processor or blender, combine all marinade ingredients except oil; process until combined. With machine running, add oil; process until smooth wet paste forms.

2 Place pork in 13x9-inch pan. Coat all sides of pork with marinade. Cover and refrigerate at least 4 hours or overnight.

3 Heat grill. Place pork on gas grill over medium heat or on charcoal grill 4 to 6 inches from medium coals. Cook 14 to 16 minutes or until internal temperature reaches 150°F., turning once. Place on cutting board.

Cover loosely with foil; let stand 10 minutes.

4 Meanwhile, in large bowl, combine zucchini and fennel. Add 1 tablespoon oil, ½ teaspoon salt and ¼ teaspoon pepper; toss to evenly coat zucchini and fennel with oil. Wrap vegetables in 2 packets of double-thickness or heavy-duty foil. Grill over medium heat 8 to 10 minutes or until vegetables are tender and lightly browned, turning once.

5 Place pork and vegetables on serving platter. Drizzle with 2 tablespoons vinegar.

TIP *Crush fennel seeds with mortar and pestle, flat side of meat mallet or bottom of saucepan.

WINE While Pinot Noir could accompany this dish, Chardonnay makes a slightly better pairing. R.H. Phillips from California is a good value, while Château Ste. Michelle "Cold Creek" from Washington State is one of the more subtle Chardonnays available.

6 servings

PER SERVING: 300 calories, 16 g total fat (3 g saturated fat), 27 g protein, 13.5 g carbohydrate, 65 mg cholesterol, 285 mg sodium, 4 g fiber

Types of Balsamic Vinegar

Shopping for a good bottle of balsamic vinegar can be a daunting task because there are no labeling standards. Not everything labeled balsamic vinegar really is. Price alone is not a reliable indicator for judging quality, so, when possible, ask for a taste, buy from a store you trust and ask sales personnel for assistance.

There are two categories of balsamic vinegar: traditional (labeled tradizionale) and commercial (sometimes labeled as condimenti or industrial).

Traditional In the provinces of Modena and Reggio Emilia, the process of making traditional balsamic vinegar has remained the same for hundreds of years. White grapes, usually Trebbiano, are pressed, producing juice called must. The must is cooked until concentrated, then aged for at least 12 years in different wood barrels.

This balsamic has the consistency of syrup. It's nearly black in color, with an extraordinary, intensely perfumed aroma. Its taste is a balance of sweet and sour. Traditional balsamic is not to be used for cooking, marinades or salad dressing. Rather, it should be used sparingly and savored. It's wonderful drizzled over aged Parmesan cheese or ripe strawberries. It's best used in small amounts, such as for finishing and garnishing your best dishes. It is the most revered balsamic, fetching prices from $60 for 100 milliliters to several hundred dollars. Two brands to look for are Del Cristo Tradizionale and Cavalli Red Seal.

Traditional
balsamic vinegar

Commercial Most balsamic vinegar available in U.S. grocery stores falls into this category. The types of commercial balsamic vinegar vary greatly in composition, however, and can include balsamic made in the traditional way but produced in areas outside Modena or Reggio Emilia; balsamic aged for fewer than 12 years; a mixture of red wine vinegar and must; or a blend of young and aged balsamic vinegar. These are the best types to use in cooking; some of them are labeled "condimenti," which usually means they are higher in quality. To ensure the vinegar you purchase was bottled in Italy, look for API MO (Modena) or API RE (Reggio Emilia) on the label. About 75 percent of commercial balsamic, however, is made from red wine vinegar with no must; instead, caramel coloring and flavor is added. This is the type you usually want to avoid.

Many bottles of balsamic carry aging claims. With commercial balsamic vinegar, however, aging is not the important aspect. (In fact, it is impossible to determine the exact age of a balsamic.) Rather, the quality of the vinegar is determined by the proportion of must to red wine vinegar and the quality of the vinegar used.

Commercial balsamic vinegar is typically priced from as little as $3 per bottle up to $30 and higher for certain brands. Use the commercial type in marinades and salad dressings, or cook the vinegar to reduce its volume and concentrate its fruit flavor for use in sauces. This is the ideal choice for braised dishes. Some brands to look for are Cavalli, Lorenza de Medici and Monari Federzoni.

Balsamic-Tossed Pasta with Fresh Tomato, Arugula and Mozzarella

Fresh garden produce and mozzarella combine with a sauce that is simply dressed with olive oil and a splash of good-quality balsamic vinegar. There is no need to cook the sauce; the heat from the pasta helps melt the cheese and warm the sauce.

2 cups chopped seeded tomatoes (2 large)
2 cups coarsely chopped arugula
2 large garlic cloves, chopped
8 oz. fresh mozzarella cheese, cut into small cubes
1 teaspoon sea salt
½ teaspoon freshly ground pepper
¼ cup extra-virgin olive oil

12 oz. strozzapreti (thin, twisted pasta) or penne
2 tablespoons balsamic vinegar

1 In large bowl, stir together tomatoes, arugula, garlic, mozzarella, salt, pepper and oil. Refrigerate 30 minutes.

2 Cook strozzapreti in large pot of boiling salted water according to package directions; drain. Toss with

Balsamic-Tossed Pasta with Fresh Tomato, Arugula and Mozzarella

sauce. Add vinegar; toss.

WINE Two wines that work with this pasta are Castello Banfi "Col di Sasso" Sangiovese-Cabernet and Castellare di Castellina Chianti Classico.

4 servings

PER SERVING: 635 calories, 29 g total fat (10 g saturated fat), 24 g protein, 72 g carbohydrate, 0 mg cholesterol, 1015 mg sodium, 4 g fiber

Balsamic-Marinated Flank Steak

Flank steak tends to be a tougher cut of meat, but the acidity in the balsamic vinegar helps tenderize it. For best results, cook it to rare to medium-rare. To carve the steak, cut it across the grain on the bias into thin slices. Thick wedges of oven-roasted potatoes are the perfect accompaniment.

- 1 (1½-lb.) flank steak
- ⅓ cup finely chopped onion
- 1 garlic clove, minced
- 3 tablespoons balsamic vinegar, divided
- 2 teaspoons olive oil
- ½ teaspoon freshly ground pepper
- ¼ teaspoon salt

1 Score both sides of flank steak in crisscross pattern, cutting ⅛ inch deep. Place in shallow glass baking dish.

2 In small bowl, stir together onion, garlic, 2 tablespoons of the vinegar, oil and pepper. Pour over steak, turning to evenly coat both sides. Cover and refrigerate at least 4 hours or overnight.

3 Heat grill. Remove and discard excess marinade from steak; sprinkle both sides with salt. Place on gas grill over medium heat or on charcoal grill 4 to 6 inches from medium coals. Cook 9 to 12 minutes or until internal temperature reaches 140°F. for medium-rare, turning once. Place on cutting board; let stand 5 minutes. Cut on diagonal into thin slices. Pour accumulated juices over slices; drizzle with remaining 1 tablespoon vinegar.

WINE A refined Cabernet Sauvignon is a fine match for the steak. Try Viña Santa Rita "120" Cabernet Sauvignon from Chile or Beaulieu Vineyard Cabernet Sauvignon from Napa.

4 servings

PER SERVING: 255 calories, 12 g total fat (4.5 g saturated fat), 34.5 g protein, .5 g carbohydrate, 90 mg cholesterol, 225 mg sodium, 0 g fiber

Shrimp Ragoût with Orzo and Feta Cheese

In this dish, balsamic vinegar is simmered with garlic and reduced to a thick syrup, which adds flavor and complexity to the shrimp ragoût. Although any small pasta may be used, sleek orzo provides just the right texture. Use fresh feta cheese packed in water instead of the dry, crumbled variety because it has a milder flavor.

- ½ cup balsamic vinegar
- 4 garlic cloves
- 2 tablespoons olive oil
- 1 cup chopped red onion
- 2 cups chopped seeded peeled tomatoes (2 large)
- 1 teaspoon finely chopped fresh thyme
- ½ teaspoon kosher (coarse) salt
- ¼ teaspoon freshly ground pepper
- 1 lb. shelled, deveined uncooked large shrimp
- 2 tablespoons chopped fresh Italian parsley
- 1½ cups orzo (rice-shaped pasta)
- 3 oz. feta cheese, diced

1 In small saucepan, combine vinegar and garlic. Bring to a simmer over medium-high heat; reduce heat to low. Cook 10 to 12 minutes or until mixture is reduced to syrup consistency. (There should be slightly less than 2 tablespoons.) Remove garlic; coarsely chop. Reserve vinegar reduction.

2 Heat oil in large skillet over medium heat. Add onion; cook 3 minutes or until softened. Stir in chopped garlic; cook 1 minute. Stir in tomatoes, thyme, salt and pepper. Bring mixture to a simmer; cook 5 minutes or until tomatoes are soft. Add shrimp. Return mixture to a simmer; cook 3 to 5 minutes or until shrimp turn pink, stirring frequently. Remove from heat; stir in vinegar reduction and parsley.

3 Meanwhile, cook orzo in large pot of boiling salted water according to package directions; drain. Place in large serving bowl. Spoon shrimp mixture over orzo; sprinkle with cheese.

4 (1¾-cup) servings

PER SERVING: 430 calories, 13.5 g total fat (4.5 g saturated fat), 28 g protein, 49.5 g carbohydrate, 180 mg cholesterol, 815 mg sodium, 3 g fiber

Jill Van Cleave is a frequent contributor to *Cooking Pleasures.*

Tandoori-Style Chicken Breasts

Stuff It

Grilled entrees get a boost from tasty fillings tucked inside.

Text and Recipes by Melanie Barnard

Maybe it has something to do with Thanksgiving, the ultimate special meal. My grandmother used to say that the turkey was really nothing more than a vehicle (albeit a tasty one) for the stuffing. Whether you believe that or not, there is and always has been a mystique associated with stuffed foods. Piping cream cheese into a celery stick transforms this most mundane vegetable into an hors d'oeuvre, and stuffing a tomato with tuna salad turns lunch into a luncheon.

In the same way, supper becomes dinner merely by stuffing the main course, from pork chops to trout. Your garden or a local farmers' market is full of natural stuffing materials — fresh herbs by the handful, tomatoes, peppers, corn, onions. The stuffings are easy to prepare, and the entrees cook quickly. These light, essence-of-summer stuffings don't need the long roasting treatment that a Thanksgiving bird requires. In fact, you don't need your oven at all because all of the cooking is done on the grill. The result is meat or fish richly seared and grilled on the outside with a burst of fresh flavors inside. The meal needs little else beyond a salad and rustic bread.

My grandmother was right. The secret to a great dinner really is in the stuffing.

Tandoori-Style Chicken Breasts

America's favorite cut of chicken is also the most difficult to grill properly. Without its natural skin and bone protection, chicken breasts can go from juicy to dry in a minute or two. A blanket of thick, seasoned yogurt provides tasty protection against overcooking and also makes a delicious crust. Stuffing the breasts with the lively flavors of lime, green onion and ginger provides a nice contrast to the mellow yogurt.

FILLING
- ¼ cup finely chopped green onions
- 2 tablespoons chopped fresh cilantro
- 1 tablespoon finely chopped fresh ginger
- 1 teaspoon grated lime peel

CHICKEN AND MARINADE
- 4 boneless skinless chicken breast halves
- 1 (8-oz.) container plain nonfat yogurt
- 2 tablespoons lime juice
- 2 large garlic cloves, minced
- 1 teaspoon ground cumin
- 1 teaspoon ground cinnamon
- 1 teaspoon ground coriander
- 1 teaspoon ground turmeric
- ½ teaspoon salt
- ¼ teaspoon cayenne pepper
- Lime wedges

1 In small bowl, stir together all filling ingredients.

2 With small sharp knife, cut pocket in each chicken breast, cutting almost to other side but not all the way through. Stuff each pocket with 1½ tablespoons filling; secure openings with toothpicks.

3 In shallow glass baking dish just large enough to hold chicken, stir together all remaining chicken and marinade ingredients except lime wedges. Place chicken in dish, turning to coat both sides. Cover; refrigerate at least 30 minutes or up to 2 hours.

4 Heat grill. Remove chicken from marinade; discard marinade. Place chicken on gas grill over medium heat or on charcoal grill 4 to 6 inches from medium coals. Grill 8 to 10 minutes or until chicken is no longer pink in center and juices run clear, turning several times. Remove toothpicks; garnish with lime wedges.

BEER/WINE The regular Samuel Adams Boston Lager is an elegant beer with a little spice that fits this dish well. A Zinfandel also holds up well to the grilling and all the spices in the chicken. Try Seghesio from Sonoma — it's flavorful without being bitter.

4 servings

PER SERVING: 160 calories, 3.5 g total fat (1 g saturated fat), 27 g protein, 3.5 g carbohydrate, 65 mg cholesterol, 145 mg sodium, .5 g fiber

Thai-Style Stuffed Steak

Thai-Style Stuffed Steak

Look for lemon grass and Thai basil in farmers' or Asian markets, or in large supermarkets. The steak can be served right off the grill or at room temperature. Accompany it with an Asian-style rice salad.

FILLING
- ⅓ cup finely chopped honey-roasted peanuts
- ¼ cup finely chopped lemon grass*
- 2 tablespoons chopped fresh Thai basil or cilantro
- 1 tablespoon fish sauce
- ¼ teaspoon crushed red pepper

MEAT AND MARINADE
- 4 (6-oz.) New York strip or filet mignon steaks (1 inch thick)
- 3 tablespoons dry sherry or apple cider
- 2 tablespoons rice wine vinegar
- 2 tablespoons fish sauce
- 1 tablespoon dark sesame oil

1 In small bowl, stir together all filling ingredients.

2 With small sharp knife, cut pocket in side of each steak, cutting almost to other side but not all the way through. Stuff each pocket with 2 tablespoons of the filling; secure openings with toothpicks.

3 In shallow glass baking dish just large enough to hold steaks, stir together sherry, vinegar, 2 tablespoons fish sauce and sesame oil. Place steaks in marinade, turning to coat both sides. Cover; refrigerate at least 2 hours or up to 8 hours, turning meat ocassionally.

4 Heat grill. Remove steaks from marinade; discard marinade. Place steaks on gas grill over medium heat or on charcoal grill 4 to 6 inches from medium coals. Grill 10 to 12 minutes for medium-rare or until of desired doneness, turning once. Remove toothpicks; serve.

TIP *If you can't find lemon grass, substitute 1 tablespoon grated lemon peel.

BEER/WINE Negra Modelo, a dark beer from Mexico, can stand up to this flavorful cut of meat. If you prefer wine, try Jekel Syrah from Monterey, California, with its ripe black-fruit character and rich body.

4 servings

PER SERVING: 320 calories, 17 g total fat (5 g saturated fat), 35 g protein, 5 g carbohydrate, 85 mg cholesterol, 425 mg sodium, 1 g fiber

Cajun Stuffed Trout

A highly seasoned Cajun vegetable dish of corn, bell pepper, onion, herbs and smoky ham makes a terrific stuffing for trout. Small-boned trout make a lovely presentation served whole, but you can ask the fishmonger to remove the heads if you wish. If you have a hinged fish grilling basket, turning the fish is a breeze. If you don't, keep the trout and filling intact by using a large spatula and turning only once during grilling.

FILLING
- 2 tablespoons butter
- 1 medium onion, chopped
- 1 small green bell pepper, chopped
- ¾ cup fresh corn kernels or frozen corn kernels, thawed

⅓ cup coarsely chopped ham (about 2 oz.)

½ teaspoon hot pepper sauce

2 tablespoons chopped fresh thyme

¼ teaspoon salt

TROUT

¼ cup yellow cornmeal

¼ teaspoon salt

¼ teaspoon freshly ground pepper

4 (8- to 10-oz.) boned whole trout

Lemon wedges

1 Melt butter in medium skillet over medium heat. Add onion, pepper, corn and ham; cook 8 to 10 minutes or until golden brown, stirring often. Stir in hot pepper sauce, thyme and ¼ teaspoon salt. Remove from heat; cool slightly. (Vegetable mixture can be made up to 8 hours ahead. Cover and refrigerate. Bring to room temperature before using.)

2 In shallow dish, stir together cornmeal, ¼ teaspoon salt and pepper. Rinse trout inside and out (do not pat dry). Stuff each trout with about ¼ cup filling; secure openings with metal skewers.* Coat both sides of trout with cornmeal mixture.

3 Heat grill; lightly oil grill rack. Place trout on gas grill over medium heat or on charcoal grill 4 to 6 inches from medium coals. Grill 10 to 12 minutes or until trout just begins to flake, turning once. Remove skewers; serve with lemon wedges.

TIP *Small metal skewers, such as those used to skewer turkey, work best in this recipe.

BEER/WINE Bass Ale is perfect here. For wine, go with Pascal Jolivet Sancerre from the Loire Valley, a full-flavored dry white that pairs nicely with the seasonings in this dish.

4 servings

PER SERVING: 380 calories, 17.5 g total fat (6 g saturated fat), 38 g protein, 16 g carbohydrate, 115 mg cholesterol, 630 mg sodium, 2.5 g fiber

Stuffing Tips

When cutting a pocket in meat or fish for stuffing, use a sharp paring knife, and take care not to cut all the way through the food or to puncture the top or bottom (lower left). To help keep the stuffing contained, make as small an opening as possible, then move the knife in and around the opening to enlarge it. Use toothpicks or small skewers (lower right) to close the opening after stuffing, but be sure to remove them before serving.

Rosemary and Feta Lamb Chops

The rosemary, garlic, olives and cheese in this stuffing are among the lush flavors that typify Provence. Serve the chops with grilled red and golden potatoes and a mixed green salad for an elegant but easy dinner party.

FILLING

½ cup (2 oz.) crumbled feta cheese

¼ cup chopped niçoise or oil-cured ripe olives

2 garlic cloves, finely chopped

2 tablespoons well-drained chopped roasted red bell peppers

1 tablespoon chopped fresh rosemary

MEAT

8 (5-oz.) loin lamb chops, 1½ inches thick

1 teaspoon olive oil

½ teaspoon salt

½ teaspoon freshly ground pepper

1 In small bowl, stir together all filling ingredients. (Filling can be made up to 4 hours ahead. Cover and refrigerate.)

2 With small sharp knife, cut large pocket in side of each chop, cutting back to bone. Stuff each pocket with about 1 tablespoon of the filling; secure openings with toothpicks. (Lamb can be stuffed up to 2 hours ahead. Cover and refrigerate.) Brush chops with oil; sprinkle with salt and pepper.

3 Heat grill. Place lamb on gas grill over medium heat or on charcoal grill 4 to 6 inches from medium coals. Grill 12 to 15 minutes for medium or until of desired doneness, turning once. Just before lamb is done cooking, turn chops on edges to grill sides. Remove toothpicks; serve.

BEER/WINE Newcastle Brown Ale is a rich, dark beer that can carry all the flavors in these lamb chops. For wine, choose either Bolla "Le Poiane" Valpolicella, which works perfectly with the rosemary, or the winery's regular Valpolicella.

4 servings

PER SERVING: 290 calories, 15.5 g total fat (6 g saturated fat), 34 g protein, 2 g carbohydrate, 115 mg cholesterol, 615 mg sodium, .5 g fiber

Panzanella-Stuffed Pork Chops

Panzanella-Stuffed Pork Chops

Panzanella is a classic Tuscan summer bread salad. The same ingredients — good day-old Italian bread, onion, garlic, basil and tomatoes — make a lovely light stuffing for pork chops.

FILLING
- ½ cup finely torn day-old Italian bread
- ½ cup seeded diced plum tomatoes
- ½ cup finely chopped sweet onion
- ¼ cup chopped fresh basil
- 2 tablespoons olive oil
- 1 tablespoon balsamic vinegar
- 3 medium garlic cloves, chopped
- ¼ teaspoon salt
- ¼ teaspoon freshly ground pepper

MEAT AND MARINADE
- 6 (8-oz.) center-cut bone-in loin pork chops, ¾ to 1 inch thick
- ½ teaspoon salt
- ¼ teaspoon freshly ground pepper
- 3 tablespoons balsamic vinegar
- 1 tablespoon olive oil

1 In small bowl, stir together all filling ingredients.

2 With small sharp knife, cut pocket in side of each chop, cutting back to bone. Stuff each pocket with 3 tablespoons of the filling; secure openings with toothpicks. Sprinkle both sides of pork with ½ teaspoon salt and ¼ teaspoon pepper.

3 In shallow dish just large enough to hold pork, stir together 3 tablespoons vinegar and 1 tablespoon oil. Place pork in dish, turning to coat both sides. Cover; refrigerate at least 15 minutes or up to 8 hours, turning once or twice.

4 Heat grill. Remove pork from marinade; discard marinade. Place pork on gas grill over medium heat or on charcoal grill 4 to 6 inches from medium coals. Grill 12 to 16 minutes or until pork is no longer pink in center, turning once. Remove toothpicks; serve.

BEER/WINE If you prefer beer, the Liberty Ale from Anchor Steam in San Francisco has an earthy quality that works. Or serve a beautiful Tuscan wine with this dish. Fattoria di Felsina Chianti Classico is an elegant red.

6 servings

Grilling Tips

When grilling stuffed entrees, avoid the temptation to flip the food every few minutes. Allow enough time on one side to sear the exterior. Then turn once and sear the other side. To make a cross-hatch pattern of grill marks, rotate the food 45 degrees halfway through cooking on one side. Turn 90 degrees to make a square crosshatch (pictured).

PER SERVING: 310 calories, 17 g total fat (5 g saturated fat), 33.5 g protein, 4.5 g carbohydrate, 95 mg cholesterol, 220 mg sodium, .5 g fiber

Melanie Barnard is a frequent contributor to Cooking Pleasures.

Sweet Potato, Pork and Sage Pot Pie

The New Pot Pie

A modern approach to an old-fashioned favorite.

Text and Recipes by Melanie Barnard

Savory fillings bubble beneath golden, flaky crusts. Rich aromas awaken appetites. These are the pleasures of pot pies, as delicious to the body as they are to the soul.

Traditional pot pies were made from leftovers — a roast turkey or beef and some boiled vegetables from an earlier meal — and the crust, from scratch. The contemporary approach relies on fresh meats and vegetables for the filling, and puff pastry for the crust. Adding high flavor ingredients, such as red wine, shiitake mushrooms, even chorizo, makes these versions just what we need: an old-fashioned favorite with modern appeal.

Sweet Potato, Pork and Sage Pot Pie

A terrific combination of seasonal flavors makes this pot pie perfect for a fall gathering. Sweet potatoes and apples lend a sweet counterpoint to savory pork.

- 1 lb. pork tenderloin, cut into 1-inch pieces
- ¾ teaspoon salt, divided
- ½ teaspoon freshly ground pepper
- 4 tablespoons all-purpose flour, divided
- 3 tablespoons vegetable oil, divided
- 1 large tart apple, such as Granny Smith, peeled, cubed (½ inch)
- 1 medium sweet potato, peeled, cubed (½ inch)*
- 1 medium onion, coarsely chopped
- 1 cup apple cider, divided
- 2 tablespoons chopped fresh sage
- ¼ cup applejack or Calvados brandy or additional cider
- ¼ cup reduced-sodium chicken broth
- 1 tablespoon cider vinegar
- 1 sheet frozen puff pastry (from 17.3-oz. pkg.), thawed
- ¼ cup (1 oz.) shredded sharp cheddar cheese
- 1 egg, beaten

1 Heat oven to 400°F. Place pork in medium bowl. Sprinkle with ½ teaspoon of the salt and pepper; toss with 1 tablespoon of the flour.

2 Heat large skillet over medium-high heat until hot. Add 1 tablespoon of the oil; heat until hot. Add pork, in batches if necessary; cook 3 to 5 minutes or until browned on all sides. Place on plate.

3 Reduce heat to medium. In same skillet, heat remaining 2 tablespoons oil until hot. Add apple, sweet potato and onion; cook 2 minutes, stirring frequently. Add ¼ cup of the cider; simmer 10 minutes or until vegetables are tender. Sprinkle with remaining 3 tablespoons flour and sage. Cook and stir 1 minute; slowly stir in remaining ¾ cup cider until smooth and bubbly. Stir in brandy, broth, vinegar and remaining ¼ teaspoon salt. Bring to a simmer; cook and stir 1 minute or until thickened and bubbly. Return pork and any accumulated juices to skillet. Spoon mixture into 8-inch (2-quart) baking dish or 6 (8-oz.) individual baking dishes.**

4 On lightly floured surface, roll puff pastry into 10-inch square. Sprinkle with cheese; lightly press into pastry

with rolling pin. Lay pastry over filling, crimping edges just inside rim of baking dish. Cut several steam slits in center of pastry; brush lightly with egg. (Pot pie can be made to this point up to 6 hours ahead. Let filling cool, then cover with pastry; refrigerate. Bake an additional 5 to 10 minutes, if necessary.)

5 Bake 25 to 30 minutes or until pastry is golden brown and filling is bubbly.

TIPS *Look for the orange-colored sweet potatoes, often labeled as yams.

**For individual baking dishes, cut puff pastry into 6 (3¼-inch) squares. Bake 20 to 25 minutes.

WINE Louis Jadot Beaujolais-Villages from France has bright fruit and enough acidity to cut through the sweetness of the potato in this pot pie. Another choice that complements the dish is a rich Chardonnay, such as Benziger from Carneros, which makes a great match with the apple and sage flavors.

6 servings

PER SERVING: 540 calories, 31.5 g total fat (10 g saturated fat), 22 g protein, 38 g carbohydrate, 80 mg cholesterol, 480 mg sodium, 2.5 g fiber

Beef and Root Vegetable Pot Pie

Beef and Root Vegetable Pot Pie

Reminiscent of pot roast, this heartwarming pie is full of old-fashioned comfort.

1 lb. beef sirloin steak, cut into 1-inch pieces
½ teaspoon salt
½ teaspoon freshly ground pepper
4 tablespoons all-purpose flour, divided

4 tablespoons butter, divided
2 cups frozen small pearl onions, thawed
1½ cups baby carrots, large pieces halved or quartered
1 medium parsnip, halved, sliced (¼ inch)

3 large garlic cloves, minced
2 tablespoons Dijon mustard
2 tablespoons chopped fresh rosemary, divided
¾ cup red wine
¾ cup reduced-sodium beef broth
1 sheet frozen puff pastry (from 17.3-oz. pkg.), thawed
1 egg, beaten

1 Heat oven to 400°F. Sprinkle beef with salt and pepper; toss with 1 tablespoon of the flour. Melt 2 tablespoons of the butter in large skillet over medium-high heat. Add beef; cook 6 minutes or until brown on all sides. Place beef on plate.

2 Melt remaining 2 tablespoons butter in same skillet over medium heat. Add onions, carrots and parsnip; cook 5 minutes or until pale brown and tender, stirring frequently. Stir in garlic. Add remaining 3 tablespoons flour; cook and stir 1 minute. Stir in mustard and 1½ tablespoons of the rosemary; slowly stir in wine and broth. Simmer, stirring occasionally, 3 minutes or until thickened and bubbly. Return beef and any accumulated juices to skillet. Spoon mixture into 8-inch (2-quart) baking dish or 6 (8-oz.) individual baking dishes.*

3 On lightly floured surface, roll puff pastry into 10-inch square. Sprinkle with remaining ½ tablespoon rosemary; lightly press into pastry with rolling pin. Lay pastry over filling, crimping edges just inside rim of baking dish. Cut several steam slits in center of pastry; brush lightly with egg. (Pot pie can be made to this point up to 6 hours ahead. Let filling cool, then cover with pastry; refrigerate. Increase baking time 5 to 10 minutes, if necessary.)

4 Bake 25 to 30 minutes or until pastry is golden brown and filling is bubbly.

TIP *For individual baking dishes, cut puff pastry into 6 (3¼-inch) squares. Bake 20 to 25 minutes.

WINE Try the juicy and fruity Les Jamelles Syrah from France. For a fuller-bodied option, try the rich and spicy Eberle Winery Steinbeck Syrah from California.

6 servings

PER SERVING: 480 calories, 30.5 g total fat (12.5 g saturated fat), 20 g protein, 30.5 g carbohydrate, 90 mg cholesterol, 480 mg sodium, 3.5 g fiber

Chorizo, Shrimp and Corn Pot Pie

Chorizo is a zesty garlic- and pepper-seasoned sausage. If you can't get chorizo, use hot Italian sausage, either pork or turkey, removing the sausage meat from the casings.

2 teaspoons cumin seeds
1 tablespoon corn oil
½ lb. chorizo, sliced (¼ inch), or bulk hot Italian sausage*
¾ cup chopped red onion
2 cups diced red, yellow and/or green bell peppers
1 cup fresh corn or frozen corn, thawed
1 chipotle chile in adobo sauce, chopped**
2 teaspoons adobo sauce
1 tablespoon yellow cornmeal
3 tablespoons all-purpose flour
1¼ cups reduced-sodium chicken broth
½ lb. shelled, deveined uncooked medium shrimp
1 sheet frozen puff pastry (from 17.3-oz. pkg.), thawed
1 egg, beaten

1 Heat oven to 400°F. In small dry skillet, toast cumin seeds over medium heat 1 minute or until slightly darker and fragrant, stirring constantly. Place on small plate.

2 In large skillet, heat oil over medium heat until hot. Add chorizo; cook 4 to 5 minutes or until browned, stirring occasionally. Place on plate. Increase heat to medium-high. Add onion, peppers and corn to drippings in skillet; cook 5 minutes or until just tender, stirring frequently. Stir in chipotle chile, adobo sauce, cornmeal and flour; cook 1 minute.

Slowly stir in broth and shrimp. Bring to a simmer; cook and stir 1 minute. (Shrimp will not be fully cooked.) Return chorizo and any accumulated juices to skillet. Spoon mixture into 8-inch (2-quart) baking dish or 6 (8-oz.) individual baking dishes.***

3 On lightly floured surface, roll puff pastry into 10-inch square. Sprinkle with cumin seeds; lightly press into pastry using rolling pin. Lay pastry over filling, crimping edges just inside rim of baking dish. Cut several steam slits in center of pastry; brush lightly with egg. (Pot pie can be made to this point up to 6 hours ahead. Let filling cool, then cover with pastry; refrigerate. Increase baking time 5 to 10 minutes, if necessary.)

4 Bake 25 to 30 minutes or until pastry is golden brown and filling is bubbly.

TIPS *Chorizo is a spicy pork sausage used in Mexican and Spanish cooking. It comes in smoked links or bulk form and can be found in the meat department of some grocery stores or Latin markets. If unavailable, substitute other highly seasoned sausage.

**Chipotle chiles are dried, smoked jalapeño chiles. They come dried, pickled or canned in adobo sauce. Look for them in the Latin section of the supermarket.

***For individual baking dishes, cut puff pastry into 6 (3¼-inch) squares. Bake 20 to 25 minutes.

WINE Rioja is a perfect match for chorizo. Try Marques de Arienzo Crianza from Spain, or add a lighter touch to the meal with Marqués de Cáceres Rosado, a very dry and refreshing alternative to red.

6 servings

PER SERVING: 540 calories, 37.5 g total fat (13 g saturated fat), 20.5 g protein, 30 g carbohydrate, 115 mg cholesterol, 835 mg sodium, 2.5 g fiber

Curried Chicken Pot Pie

Curried Chicken Pot Pie

You'll love the blend of flavors in this Indian-inspired pot pie. The curry powder plays an important role in the pie's flavor, so be sure yours is fresh and high quality.

1 lb. boneless skinless chicken thighs or breasts, cut into 1-inch pieces

½ teaspoon salt
¼ teaspoon cayenne pepper
3 tablespoons all-purpose flour, divided
2 tablespoons butter, divided
1½ cups coarsely chopped onion
1 small red bell pepper, cut into ½-inch pieces
1½ tablespoons curry powder
1 tablespoon minced fresh ginger
2 medium red potatoes, cut into ½-inch pieces

1 cup reduced-sodium chicken broth
2½ cups broccoli florets
2 cups cauliflower florets
½ cup unsweetened coconut milk
1 tablespoon lime juice
1 sheet frozen puff pastry (from 17.3-oz. pkg.), thawed
2 tablespoons chopped fresh cilantro
1 egg, beaten

1 Heat oven to 400°F. Sprinkle chicken with salt, cayenne and 1 tablespoon of the flour.

2 In large skillet, melt 1½ tablespoons of the butter over medium-high heat. Add chicken; cook 5 minutes or until brown on all sides, turning once. Place on plate. Melt remaining ½ tablespoon butter in same skillet; add onion and bell pepper. Cook 4 minutes or just until softened, stirring frequently. Sprinkle with remaining 2 tablespoons flour, curry powder and ginger. Cook, stirring, 1 minute. Stir in potatoes and chicken broth. Bring to a simmer; cook 1 minute, stirring constantly. Cover; simmer 4 minutes. Stir in broccoli, cauliflower, coconut milk and lime juice. Return chicken and any accumulated juices to skillet. Spoon mixture into shallow 8-inch (2-quart) baking dish or 6 (8-oz.) individual baking dishes.*

3 On lightly floured surface, roll puff pastry into 10-inch square. Sprinkle with cilantro; lightly press into pastry using rolling pin. Lay pastry over filling, crimping edges just inside rim of baking dish. Cut several steam slits in center of pastry; brush lightly with egg. (Pot pie can be made to this point up to 6 hours ahead. Let filling cool, then cover with pastry; refrigerate. Increase baking time 5 to 10 minutes, if necessary.)

4 Bake 25 to 30 minutes or until pastry is golden brown and filling is bubbly.

TIP *For individual baking dishes, cut puff pastry into 6 (3¼-inch) squares. Bake 20 to 25 minutes.

6 servings

PER SERVING: 540 calories, 33.5 g total fat (15 g saturated fat), 23.5 g protein, 37 g carbohydrate, 90 mg cholesterol, 480 mg sodium, 4.5 g fiber

Melanie Barnard is a frequent contributor to The Cooking Club of America's library of cookbooks.

Working with Puff Pastry

Pot pies can be topped with various crusts, including pie pastry, biscuits and puff pastry. The easiest and fastest one to use, however, is ready-made puff pastry.

Puff pastry is dough that has been rolled with layers of butter. As the dough bakes, the butter releases steam, creating dozens of puffy layers of pastry.

- If the pastry is frozen, thaw it according to the package directions. Work quickly when using it. It should not become warm; if it does, the layers will not rise properly.

- When rolling puff pastry, work from the center of the dough toward the edges, keeping the thickness as consistent as possible to achieve an even rise in the oven.

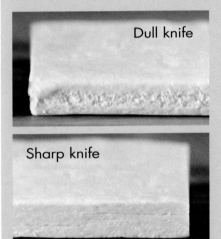

Dull knife

Sharp knife

- Cut the rolled pastry with a very sharp knife. If you use a dull knife, the cut edges stick together and won't rise properly.

- The pastry can be rolled to fit various shapes of baking dishes or cut into pieces for individual dishes. Dough scraps can be cut into whimsical shapes with a small cookie or canapé cutter and baked separately or with the crust.

- After placing the dough over the filling, loosely fit the edges just inside the rim of the baking dish. When you brush on the egg glaze, be careful not to glue the edges of the dough to the sides of the dish.

- Make several slashes in the top of the pastry with a sharp knife. These allow steam to escape during baking and promote even rising in the center.

- It's important to bake puff pastry in a very hot oven, at least 400°F. for maximum rise. This also allows the filling to heat thoroughly in about the same amount of time it takes the pastry to become golden, flaky and puffed.

Fitting the edges

Fresh Ginger Roulade

Fluted Strawberry-Rhubarb Tarts

Spiced Apple Cake with
Cranberries and Nuts

Fresh Cranberry-
Studded Bread Pudding

Desserts

Blackberry Meringue Bars

Golden Gingerbread People

The Joy of Ginger

Put some spice into your life during the holidays.

Text and Recipes by Alice Medrich

It starts with an alluring fragrance. The heady aromas compel you to take that first bite, then it's a long, lingering kiss of sweet and spicy flavors. Time and again, ginger beckons. Whether it's the hot bite of fresh ginger or the earthy aroma of ground ginger, it's an irresistible pleasure that never disappoints. It's as cozy as a cup of tea with a longtime lover and as seductive as an exotic stranger. And it's the star in every one of these desserts.

Golden Gingerbread People

These spicy cookies are fun to decorate with a ginger-flavored icing, or even plain or lemon-flavored melted white chocolate. For ease in rolling and cutting, make the dough the night before and chill.

GINGERBREAD
2¼ cups all-purpose flour
¼ teaspoon salt
¾ teaspoon baking soda
2 teaspoons ground ginger
1½ teaspoons cinnamon
½ teaspoon ground allspice
⅔ cup packed brown sugar
⅔ cup sugar
½ cup unsalted butter, melted, warm
¼ cup light molasses
2 teaspoons grated fresh ginger
1 egg

FROSTING
1 cup powdered sugar
¼ teaspoon finely grated fresh ginger
1 to 2 tablespoons water

1 In medium bowl, combine flour, salt, baking soda, ground ginger, cinnamon and allspice. In large bowl, stir together brown sugar, sugar, butter, molasses, fresh ginger and egg until well blended. Slowly stir in flour mixture until just combined. Form dough into 2 flat rounds. Cover and refrigerate at least overnight or up to 3 days.

2 Place oven racks in upper and lower thirds of oven; heat oven to 350°F. (If baking only one sheet of cookies at a time, place rack in center of oven.) Line 2 baking sheets with parchment paper.

3 Lightly sprinkle surface with flour. Roll 1 dough round to ⅛-inch thickness. Use cookie cutters to cut dough into people. Remove and reserve dough scraps from around each cookie. Place cookies at least 1 inch apart on baking sheets. Bake 7 to 9 minutes or until cookies just begin to color at edges, switching baking sheet positions halfway through baking. Cool completely on wire rack. Repeat with remaining dough and dough scraps.

4 In small bowl, stir together powdered sugar, ¼ teaspoon fresh ginger and 1 tablespoon of the water; add additional water ½ teaspoon at a time, if necessary. Decorate cookies with frosting.

About 5½ dozen (2½-inch) cookies

PER COOKIE: 55 calories, 1.5 g total fat (1 g saturated fat), .5 g protein, 10.5 g carbohydrate, 5 mg cholesterol, 25 mg sodium, 0 g fiber

Crystallized Ginger

It's easy to find crystallized ginger in most stores, but you also can make your own. The recipe is very simple, although it requires time. Two 10-minute blanchings in lightly sweetened water work to cook and soften the fibers. Then the ginger pieces are simmered three times for only 5 minutes in heavier syrup, with an hour of cooling and infusing after each.

8 oz. young or baby ginger
2¼ cups sugar, divided
4¾ cups water, divided

1 With vegetable peeler, peel ginger. Slice across grain into ⅛- to ¼-inch-thick rounds (you will have about 1 cup ginger). Place in medium saucepan with ¼ cup of the sugar and 2 cups of the water. Bring to a boil over medium-high heat. Reduce heat to low; simmer 10 minutes.

2 Drain; return ginger to pot. Add ¼ cup of the sugar and 2 cups of the water; simmer 10 minutes.

3 Drain; return ginger to pot. Add 1½ cups of the sugar and remaining ¾ cup of the water. Bring to a simmer, stirring occasionally. Remove sugar from sides of pot with wet brush. Simmer without stirring 5 minutes.

4 Turn off heat; let ginger cool in syrup at least 1 hour. (Do not worry if some syrup crystallizes as it cools.) Without stirring, bring mixture to a simmer over medium heat; simmer 5 minutes. Cool ginger in syrup at least 1 hour. Again, bring to a simmer over medium heat; simmer 5 minutes. (If syrup reaches more than 238°F. and thickens like candy, add a few tablespoons of water to thin it.)

5 Spread remaining ¼ cup sugar on plate. With slotted spoon, remove ginger from syrup; discard syrup. Place ginger on sugar. Turn to coat with sugar. Allow to air dry several hours before storing. Store in airtight container.

TIP For a milder flavor and more

candied texture, simmer the ginger an additional one or two times. Add about 3 tablespoons water to syrup each time before reheating to compensate for evaporation.

About 1 cup

PER ¼ CUP: 120 calories, 0 g total fat (0 g saturated fat), 0 g protein, 30 g carbohydrate, 0 mg cholesterol, 20 mg sodium, 0 g fiber

Fresh Ginger Roulade

Here's a sophisticated company dessert that is simple to make. Light and tender as a soufflé, the cake is loaded with fresh, hot-on-the-palate ginger and filled with soothing, lightly sweetened whipped cream.

CAKE
1¼ cups all-purpose flour
1 teaspoon baking soda
¼ teaspoon salt
¼ cup packed light brown sugar
¼ cup light molasses
¼ cup dark corn syrup
2 egg yolks
½ cup unsalted butter, melted, warm
½ cup finely minced fresh ginger*
2 tablespoons water
3 egg whites, room temperature
⅛ teaspoon cream of tartar
¼ cup sugar
Powdered sugar

FILLING
1⅓ cups whipping cream
     or crème fraîche
1 teaspoon vanilla
½ teaspoon grated fresh ginger
4 teaspoons sugar

1 Heat oven to 350°F. Spray 17x12x1-inch pan with nonstick cooking spray. Line with parchment paper; spray with nonstick cooking spray.

2 In medium bowl, stir together flour, baking soda and salt. In large bowl, whisk together brown sugar, molasses, corn syrup, egg yolks, melted butter, minced ginger and water. Stir in flour mixture just until incorporated.

3 In large bowl, beat egg whites and cream of tartar at medium-high speed until soft peaks form. Gradually add ¼ cup sugar, beating until egg whites are stiff but not dry. Fold one-fourth of the egg whites into flour mixture. Fold in remaining egg whites. Pour batter into pan; gently spread evenly.

4 Bake 10 to 12 minutes or until toothpick inserted in center comes out clean.

5 While cake is baking, place clean dish towel on work surface; sprinkle with enough powdered sugar to lightly coat towel. Remove cake from oven; immediately turn cake out onto prepared towel. Peel off parchment paper. Roll up cake lengthwise with towel, starting with short edge. Let stand to cool.

6 Meanwhile, in large bowl, beat

Fresh Ginger Roulade

cream, vanilla and grated ginger at medium-high speed just until thickened. Add 4 teaspoons sugar; beat at medium-high speed just until stiff peaks form (do not overbeat).

7 When cake is cool, unroll. Spread evenly with cream. Roll up cake, starting at short edge. Wrap log in foil; refrigerate at least 2 hours or until ready to serve. To serve, unwrap roulade; transfer to serving platter. If desired, sift additional powdered sugar over top. Store in refrigerator.

TIP *To eliminate long pieces of fiber, peel ginger and slice it across the grain in thin (1/4-inch or thinner) coins before mincing it.

WINE A delicate dessert wine, such as Markham Muscat from Napa or Quady Essensia, is the perfect accompaniment to the ginger in this dessert.

12 servings

PER SERVING: 295 calories, 17 g total fat (10 g saturated fat), 3.5 g protein, 33.5 g carbohydrate, 85 mg cholesterol, 195 mg sodium, .5 g fiber

Caramelized Ginger-Hazelnut Tart

Ginger teams with hazelnuts in this crunchy, rich, wonderfully decadent tart. A combination of fresh and crystallized ginger is the secret to the snappy flavor.

CRUST
- 1/2 cup unsalted butter, melted
- 2 tablespoons sugar
- 1/8 teaspoon salt
- 1 tablespoon water
- 1/2 teaspoon vanilla
- 1 cup all-purpose flour

FILLING
- 2/3 cup sugar
- 2/3 cup heavy whipping cream
- 1 cup chopped hazelnuts (4 oz.)
- 1/4 cup finely chopped crystallized ginger
- 2 teaspoons grated fresh ginger
- 1 tablespoon brandy or rum, if desired
- 1 oz. bittersweet chocolate, chopped

1 Heat oven to 350°F. In medium bowl, combine butter, 2 tablespoons sugar, salt, water and vanilla. Mix in flour just until absorbed (dough will be very soft and moist). Press dough in bottom and up sides of 9 1/2-inch tart pan. (Do not prick crust.) Place on baking sheet. Bake 10 to 15 minutes or until crust is set but not brown. Cool completely on wire rack. Increase oven temperature to 400°F.

2 Meanwhile, in medium saucepan, bring 2/3 cup sugar and cream to a boil over medium-high heat. Remove from heat; stir in hazelnuts, crystallized ginger, fresh ginger and brandy. Cool 15 minutes.

3 Place tart pan with crust on

Caramelized Ginger-Hazelnut Tart

baking sheet. Pour filling into crust, evenly distributing nuts and ginger. Cover crust with foil. Bake at 400°F. for 30 to 35 minutes or until filling is pale caramel color with patches of lighter cream color. (Filling will bubble up during baking, then settle down while cooling.)

4 Cool on wire rack, loosening rim of tart pan several times as tart cools to prevent crust from sticking to pan.

5 In microwave-safe bowl, melt chocolate on high 30 to 40 seconds or until soft; stir until chocolate is smooth. Drizzle over tart. Serve tart at room temperature.

WINE Hazelnuts are a natural pairing with tawny port. Both the Sandeman Tawny Port and the richer Dow Boardroom Tawny work well and aren't overly sweet.

8 servings

PER SERVING: 425 calories, 28 g total fat (12.5 g saturated fat), 4 g protein, 41.5 g carbohydrate, 55 mg cholesterol, 60 mg sodium, 1.5 g fiber

Ginger-Cranberry Ring

Serve this cake with coffee or tea any time of day, including breakfast. Double the recipe and make an extra for the freezer or to give.

¾ cup dried cranberries
¼ cup cognac, brandy or
    apple juice
⅓ cup buttermilk, room temperature
1 teaspoon vanilla
¾ cup pecan halves

Ginger-Cranberry Ring

1 1/4 cups all-purpose flour
1/4 teaspoon baking powder
1/4 teaspoon baking soda
1/4 teaspoon salt
1/2 cup unsalted butter, softened
1 cup sugar
2 eggs, room temperature, beaten
1/2 cup diced crystallized ginger
GLAZE
1/4 cup unsalted butter, melted, warm
2 cups powdered sugar
1 teaspoon ground ginger
3 to 4 tablespoons milk or cream

1 In medium glass measuring cup, combine cranberries and cognac. Let stand 15 minutes; stir in buttermilk and vanilla.
2 Meanwhile, heat oven to 325°F. Grease and flour 6-cup (8 1/2-inch) kugelhopf pan or 6-cup Bundt pan.
3 Spread pecans on baking sheet; bake 8 to 10 minutes or until fragrant and lightly colored. Cool completely. Chop until size of cranberries.
4 In medium bowl, stir together flour, baking powder, baking soda and salt. In large bowl, beat butter at medium speed until creamy. Add sugar; beat at medium-high speed 4 minutes or until light and fluffy.
5 Add eggs to butter mixture, beating at medium speed 2 minutes. At low speed, alternately add flour and cranberry mixture to butter mixture, beginning and ending with flour mixture. Stir in ginger and pecans.
6 Spoon batter into pan, spreading evenly. Bake 55 to 60 minutes or until toothpick inserted in center comes out clean. Cool in pan on wire rack 10 minutes. Invert cake onto wire rack; cool completely. (Cake can be made up to 3 days ahead and refrigerated. Or freeze up to 3 months.)
7 In medium bowl, whisk together all glaze ingredients until smooth and creamy; spoon over cake.
12 servings

PER SERVING: 400 calories, 17.5 g total fat (8 g saturated fat), 3.5 g protein, 60.5 g carbohydrate, 65 mg cholesterol, 125 mg sodium, 1.5 g fiber

Alice Medrich is a pastry chef and cookbook author based in Berkeley, California.

The Many Faces of Ginger

Ginger is available in a variety of forms. Each has a unique flavor, and they vary in how they're used in cooking. Three types of ginger are typically used in baking — crystallized ginger, fresh ginger and ground ginger.

Crystallized Ginger This is ginger that has been cooked in a sugar syrup and coated with sugar. It can be chopped and used as an ingredient, like raisins or chocolate chips, in baked goods. Crystallized ginger that has been diced is sometimes sold as "ginger chips."

Fresh Ginger, or Gingerroot Fresh ginger is actually the knobby rhizome, or underground stem, of the ginger plant. It has a brown, papery skin. Look for taut, smooth skin with a light sheen. Fresh ginger should be heavy for its size. If it's lightweight or shriveled, it has lost a lot of its natural moisture and will be less flavorful. Mature ginger is yellow-green in color and has a spicy, pungent flavor and slightly sweet aroma. It has a fibrous texture, and its skin is somewhat tough and should be peeled. Young ginger, or baby ginger, looks fresh and moist with a lighter color and has a more delicate flavor and a paper-thin skin that may or may not be peeled. Fresh ginger can be stored for about a week, unwrapped, in a cool dry place, as you would a potato. It will keep for several weeks if you store it in the vegetable bin of the refrigerator. Wrap it in a paper towel to absorb moisture that might produce mold, and then put it in a plastic bag. Some cooks like to freeze whole ginger and grate it as needed. Ginger should be peeled with a vegetable peeler before slicing, grating or pureeing it. To eliminate unpleasantly long fibers, slice ginger thinly across the grain before chopping, mincing or pureeing it. You may add fresh ginger to recipes that call for ground dried ginger. It adds pungency and perks up the flavor.

Ground Ginger This familiar yellow powder is very pungent with an earthy aroma. It's traditionally used to flavor baked goods, such as cookies, pies and cakes, as well as savory foods. It's recommended that you not substitute dried ginger for fresh ginger in recipes.

Fluted Strawberry-Rhubarb Tarts

Spring Fling

Indulge in the season's bright, fresh flavors with these sweet offerings.

Recipes by Carolyn Weil

Thank goodness for lemons, mint, strawberries and rhubarb. They're our first taste of fresh-from-the-garden fruits, a happy shift from the limited offerings we've had for months. All are available early in the year, and their flavors, alone or together, brighten any occasion. Lemon's color and zesty flavor perfectly complement delicate, aromatic mint. And the classic contrast of sweet strawberries and tart rhubarb never disappoints our winter-weary palates.

Cakes and tarts are the perfect way to showcase these spring standards. Kept simple but classic, these desserts are flavorful but not fussy. They're perfect for entertaining and a delightful way to move into the lighter foods that come with the change in seasons.

Fluted Strawberry-Rhubarb Tarts

Although these scrumptious tarts have a free-form look, they are actually baked in individual tart pans. The pans help the tarts hold their shape so the ruffled crusts don't unfold during baking.

CRUST
- ¾ cup unsalted butter, softened
- 6 oz. cream cheese, softened
- 1¾ cups all-purpose flour
- 2 tablespoons sugar
- ¼ teaspoon salt

FILLING
- 1½ cups thinly sliced rhubarb
- 1½ cups quartered strawberries
- ¾ cup sugar
- 2 tablespoons all-purpose flour
- Dash salt
- 1½ tablespoons unsalted butter

1 In large bowl, beat butter and cream cheese at medium speed until smooth. Add all remaining crust ingredients; mix until dough pulls together. Pat into 4-inch round; cover and refrigerate 1 hour.
2 Heat oven to 375°F. Roll out dough to ⅛-inch thickness. Cut 6 (6-inch) circles from dough.* Line bottom and sides of 6 (4-inch) fluted tart pans with dough. (Dough edges will stick up above rims of pans.) Place tart pans on baking sheet.
3 In large bowl, toss together rhubarb, strawberries, ¾ cup sugar, 2 tablespoons flour and dash salt. Divide fruit mixture evenly among tart pans. Fold edges of dough over filling, pinching and overlapping edges. Dot each tart with butter.
4 Place tart pans with baking sheet in oven. Bake 10 minutes. Reduce oven temperature to 350°F.; bake an additional 25 to 35 minutes or until golden brown. Cool on wire rack; remove from pans.
TIP *Using bowl or cup with 6-inch diameter as guide, trace and cut template out of paper plate to use for making 6-inch rounds.
6 servings

PER SERVING: 595 calories, 36.5 g total fat (22.5 g saturated fat), 7 g protein, 63.5 g carbohydrate, 100 mg cholesterol, 230 mg sodium, 2.5 g fiber

Lemon-Mint Meringue Cake

A take-off on lemon meringue pie, this luscious cake has an added flavor twist. The sponge cake layers are soaked with a fresh mint syrup, a delightful complement to the tart lemon filling.

CAKE
- 6 eggs, separated
- ¼ cup unsalted butter, melted, cooled slightly
- 2 teaspoons vanilla
- 1 cup sugar
- 1 cup cake flour, divided

SYRUP
- ½ cup water
- ½ cup sugar
- ½ cup loosely packed mint leaves

FILLING
- 3 egg yolks
- 1 egg
- ½ cup sugar
- ½ cup lemon juice
- 2 tablespoons grated lemon peel
- Dash salt
- ¼ cup unsalted butter, cut up

MERINGUE
- 3 egg whites
- 1 cup sugar
- ¼ cup water
- ¼ teaspoon cream of tartar

1 Heat oven to 350°F. Spray 9x2-inch round cake pan with nonstick cooking spray; line bottom with parchment paper. In small bowl, whisk together 6 egg yolks, melted butter and vanilla.
2 In large bowl, beat 6 egg whites at high speed until soft peaks form. Gradually add 1 cup sugar. Beat 3 minutes or until shiny, stiff peaks form.

Lemon-Mint Meringue Cake

3 Pour yolk mixture over egg white mixture; immediately sift ¹/₂ cup of the flour over eggs. Gently fold together. Sift remaining ¹/₂ cup flour over batter; fold in, being careful not to deflate egg whites.

4 Pour batter into pan. Bake 30 to 40 minutes or until golden brown and toothpick inserted in center comes out clean. Cool completely on wire rack.

5 Place all syrup ingredients in small saucepan. Bring to a boil over medium-high heat, stirring occasionally. Remove from heat; let stand until cool. Strain out mint leaves.

6 Place sieve over medium bowl. In heavy medium saucepan, whisk together 3 egg yolks (reserve whites for meringue), 1 egg and ¹/₂ cup

sugar until smooth. Whisk in lemon juice, lemon peel and salt. Add butter. Cook over medium to medium-low heat 7 to 9 minutes or until slightly thick and temperature reaches 160°F., stirring constantly. Do not boil.

7 Immediately strain through sieve into bowl. Place plastic wrap directly on surface to prevent film from forming. Refrigerate 2 hours or until completely cool.

8 When cake is cool, remove from pan; slice horizontally into 3 layers. To assemble cake, place one layer on 9-inch cardboard round or removable bottom of 9-inch tart pan. Brush with one-third of the syrup; spread generous ¹/₂ cup of the filling over cake. Place second cake layer on filling. Brush with one-third of the

syrup; spread with remaining filling. Top with third cake layer. Brush with remaining syrup. Place on baking sheet; refrigerate while preparing meringue.

9 Heat oven to 400°F. In large bowl, whisk together all meringue ingredients. Place bowl over saucepan of simmering water (do not let bowl touch water). Beat at high speed 6 to 8 minutes or until meringue quadruples in volume and becomes stiff and glossy. Immediately spread over assembled cake. Bake cake on baking sheet at 400° F. for 5 to 7 minutes or until meringue is golden brown. (Cake can be made up to 6 hours ahead. Refrigerate.) Store in refrigerator.
WINE A delicate Muscat, with its peach and honey flavors, is recommended

Strawberries and Cream Cake

here. Both Markham and Quady Essencia Orange Muscat from Napa Valley are sumptuous dessert wines that are light and not overly sweet.

12 servings

PER SERVING: 360 calories, 12 g total fat (6 g saturated fat), 6 g protein, 58.5 g carbohydrate, 200 mg cholesterol, 105 mg sodium, 0 g fiber

Strawberries and Cream Cake

This delicate cake makes a showy presentation yet is fairly simple to make. Follow the folding directions carefully to ensure light, airy cake layers.

CAKE
- 6 eggs, separated
- ¼ cup unsalted butter, melted, cooled slightly
- ½ teaspoon almond extract
- 1 cup sugar
- ¾ cup cake flour, divided
- ¼ cup sliced almonds, toasted, ground*

CREAM
- 2 cups heavy whipping cream, chilled
- 2 tablespoons sugar
- ½ teaspoon almond extract

STRAWBERRIES
- 2 cups sliced strawberries, divided
- 12 whole strawberries for garnish, halved

1 Heat oven to 350°F. Spray 9x2-inch round cake pan with nonstick cooking spray; line bottom with parchment paper. In small bowl, whisk together egg yolks, butter and almond extract.

2 In large bowl, beat egg whites at high speed until soft peaks form. Gradually add 1 cup sugar in a steady stream. Beat 3 minutes or until shiny, stiff peaks form.

3 Pour yolk mixture over egg white mixture; immediately sift about half of the flour over eggs. Gently fold together. Sift remaining half flour over batter; fold in. Fold in almonds, being careful not to deflate egg whites.

4 Pour batter into pan. Bake 30 to 40 minutes or until golden brown and toothpick inserted in center comes out clean. Cool on wire rack.

5 Meanwhile, in large bowl, beat all cream ingredients at medium-high speed until stiff peaks form.

6 When cake is cool, remove from pan; slice horizontally into 3 layers. To assemble cake, place one layer on

9-inch cardboard round or cake platter. Spread with 1 cup cream; cover with 1 cup of the sliced strawberries. Place second cake layer on strawberries. Spread with 1 cup cream; cover with remaining 1 cup strawberries. Top with third cake layer; spread sides and top with remaining cream. Decorate top with halved strawberries. Store in refrigerator.

TIP *To toast almonds, place on baking sheet; bake at 375°F. for 6 minutes or until deep golden brown.

WINE A slightly sweet rosé, such as Zaca Mesa "Z Gris", or a dessert sparkler, such as Schramsberg Crément from Napa Valley, has the necessary sweetness to match this dish without being cloying.

12 servings

PER SERVING: 310 calories, 20 g total fat (11 g saturated fat), 5 g protein, 29 g carbohydrate, 160 mg cholesterol, 70 mg sodium, 1.5 g fiber

Cream Cheese Pound Cake with Rhubarb

Cream cheese lends superb flavor and texture to this moist, tender pound cake. For the prettiest cake, use bright red rhubarb stalks; green stalks will turn brown during baking.

    3 cups all-purpose flour
    2 teaspoons baking powder
    1 teaspoon salt
    1 cup unsalted butter,
       softened
    1 (8-oz.) pkg. cream cheese,
       softened
    3 cups sugar
    8 eggs, room temperature*
 1½ tablespoons grated orange
       peel
    1 tablespoon vanilla
    2 cups thinly sliced rhubarb
GLAZE
 1½ cups powdered sugar
 1½ tablespoons orange juice

1 Heat oven to 325°F. Place oven rack in lower third of oven. Spray 12-cup Bundt pan with nonstick cooking spray; sprinkle lightly with flour. In medium bowl, stir together flour, baking powder and salt.

2 In large bowl, beat butter and cream cheese at medium-high speed until light and fluffy. Add sugar; continue beating 3 to 4 minutes or until pale.

3 In another large bowl, whisk together eggs, orange peel and vanilla. Add half of egg mixture to butter mixture; mix well. At low speed, beat in remaining half egg mixture. Slowly mix in flour mixture; fold in rhubarb.

4 Pour batter into pan. Bake 65 to 75 minutes or until golden brown and toothpick inserted in center comes out clean. Cool on wire rack 15 minutes. Remove from pan; cool completely.

5 Meanwhile, in medium bowl, stir together all glaze ingredients until smooth. When cake is cool, drizzle with glaze.

TIP *To warm eggs quickly, place whole eggs in bowl of hot water. Let stand 5 to 10 minutes.

12 servings

PER SERVING: 625 calories, 25.5 g total fat (15 g saturated fat), 9 g protein, 90.5 g carbohydrate, 205 mg cholesterol, 375 mg sodium, 1 g fiber

Lemon Cream Tart

This gem features a silky, tart lemon filling. Like Key lime pie, it's made with sweetened condensed milk, so it requires no additional sugar. Try it with Meyer lemons in the early part of the year when they are in season.

CRUST
  ½ cup unsalted butter,
       softened
    4 oz. cream cheese, softened
 1¼ cups all-purpose flour
 1½ tablespoons sugar
  ⅛ teaspoon salt
FILLING
    4 egg yolks
    1 tablespoon grated lemon
       peel
    1 (14-oz.) can sweetened
       condensed milk
  ½ cup fresh lemon juice

CREAM
    1 cup heavy whipping cream
    1 tablespoon sugar
    1 teaspoon vanilla
GARNISH
    Crystallized Mint Leaves
    (page 119)

1 In large bowl, beat butter and cream cheese at medium speed 1 minute or until smooth. Add all remaining crust ingredients. Beat 30 seconds or just until dough forms. Pat into 4-inch round; cover and refrigerate 1 hour.

2 Place oven rack in lower third of oven. Heat oven to 375°F. Roll out dough to 11-inch round. Line bottom and sides of 9-inch tart pan with dough; trim excess. Refrigerate 15 minutes.

3 Line dough with foil; fill with 1 cup pie weights or dried beans. Bake 20 minutes. Remove foil and pie weights; bake an additional 10 to 15 minutes or until light golden brown.

4 Meanwhile, in medium bowl, whisk together egg yolks and lemon peel until mixture is light colored; add sweetened condensed milk and lemon juice, whisking well after each addition. Pour into partially baked crust; bake 12 to 14 minutes or until filling is set. Cool completely on wire rack.

5 In medium bowl, beat all cream ingredients at medium-high speed until stiff peaks form. Fill pastry bag fitted with star tip or resealable plastic bag with corner cut off with cream. Decorate tart with cream; garnish with Crystallized Mint Leaves. Store in refrigerator.

8 servings

PER SERVING: 515 calories, 31 g total fat (18.5 g saturated fat), 9.5 g protein, 51.5 g carbohydrate, 200 mg cholesterol, 225 mg sodium, .5 g fiber

Cooking instructor Carolyn Weil, from Berkeley, California, has more than 20 years' experience as a professional baker.

Folding Egg Whites

Sponge-style cakes, such as *Lemon-Mint Meringue Cake* (page 115) and *Strawberries and Cream Cake* (page 117), are light and airy in texture. The cakes owe their texture to beaten egg whites and sugar that are folded with egg yolks and flour. The cakes' leavening, or rising power, comes entirely from the egg whites, so the step of folding the egg whites is critical. If you mix the batter too much when folding, the eggs will deflate and you'll have a flat cake.

Crystallized Mint Leaves

To paint the mint leaves, use a small craft paintbrush that's reserved for this purpose alone.

1 After the egg whites and sugar have been beaten to stiff but not dry peaks, add the egg yolk mixture and half of the flour. To keep the mixture light and airy, add the flour using a sieve or sifter.

2 To fold the mixture together, bring a rubber spatula straight down into the mixture and slide it across the bottom of the bowl, bringing it up the side and turning over the mixture. Move the bowl one-quarter turn and repeat the process until most of the flour has been incorporated. Not all of the flour will be completely mixed in — this is okay.

3 Sift the remaining flour over the mixture, and repeat the folding process. This is a gentle process in which you're trying to keep as much air in the egg mixture as possible, so you want to be careful not to overmix. When you're finished, the batter should be light and airy; there may even be a few traces of flour or egg white that are not mixed in. If you overmix, your cake may stay flat and not rise.

1 tablespoon meringue
    powder*
3 tablespoons water
16 to 20 fresh mint leaves
    Superfine sugar

1 Line baking sheet with parchment or waxed paper.

2 In small bowl, whisk together meringue powder and water until foamy. Working with 1 leaf at a time, gently paint each side of leaf with thin layer of mixture. Sprinkle both sides with sugar; place on baking sheet. Repeat with remaining leaves. Let dry at room temperature at least 3 hours or up to 24 hours. (Leaves can be made up to 1 day ahead. Store in airtight plastic container.)

TIP *Meringue powder usually can be found wherever cake decorating supplies are sold.

Spiced Apple Cake with Cranberries and Nuts

Any Day Cakes

Olive oil makes rich and moist homestyle cakes.

Text and Recipes by Susan G. Purdy

Cakes made with oil are a much-loved American tradition. Who can resist a luscious piece of carrot, apple or zucchini cake? Oil is the secret to their rich, moist crumb. It also helps them stay fresh for an extended time.

Mediterranean cooks make cakes with oil, too, but they use olive oil. Not only does it make a moist cake, it's a heart-healthy choice for fat. It has higher levels of good fats, and it can lower levels of bad fats.

For baking, the trick is to pick the right type of oil. Cold-pressed extra-light olive oil gives you all the benefits of olive oil without a trace of olive taste or aroma. Try it out with these rich, homey cakes. You just might find some new favorites — in the cakes and the olive oil.

Spiced Apple Cake with Cranberries and Nuts

This rich, moist cake combines all the flavors of late summer and early fall. You can bake it in advance and freeze it for easy entertaining. Serve the cake topped with the glaze and chopped nuts, or just sift on a little powdered sugar.

CAKE
- 3 cups all-purpose flour
- ½ teaspoon baking powder
- ½ teaspoon baking soda
- ¾ teaspoon salt
- ½ teaspoon ground cinnamon
- ½ teaspoon ground nutmeg
- ½ teaspoon ground allspice
- ½ teaspoon ground ginger
- 3 large apples (Gala, Golden Delicious or Granny Smith), peeled, cut into ½-inch pieces (3 cups)
- 1 cup dried cranberries or raisins
- 1 cup coarsely chopped walnuts
- 1½ cups extra-light or mild olive oil
- 2 cups sugar
- 2 teaspoons vanilla
- 3 tablespoons milk
- 3 eggs

GLAZE
- 1¾ cups powdered sugar
- ¼ teaspoon ground cinnamon
- 2 to 3 tablespoons milk
- 1 tablespoon light corn syrup
- ½ teaspoon vanilla
- ¼ cup chopped walnuts

1 Heat oven to 350°F. Grease 9½x3-inch plain tube pan with shortening. Sprinkle with flour; tap sides of pan to remove excess.
2 In medium bowl, whisk together flour, baking powder, baking soda, salt, ½ teaspoon cinnamon, nutmeg, allspice and ginger until blended. In large bowl, toss together apples, cranberries, 1 cup walnuts and ¼ cup of the flour mixture.
3 In another large bowl, beat oil, sugar, 2 teaspoons vanilla, milk and eggs at medium speed until well-blended. Reduce speed to low; beat in remaining flour mixture just until moistened. Stir in apple mixture until well-blended.
4 Spoon batter into pan. Bake 1 hour 15 minutes to 1 hour 20 minutes or until golden brown and toothpick inserted in center comes out clean. Cool on wire rack 20 minutes. Invert onto wire rack; cool completely.
5 Meanwhile, in medium bowl, whisk powdered sugar, ¼ teaspoon cinnamon, 2 tablespoons milk, corn syrup and ½ teaspoon vanilla until smooth, adding additional milk, if necessary. Drizzle over cake; sprinkle with chopped walnuts.

12 servings

PER SERVING: 725 calories, 36.5 g total fat (5 g saturated fat), 7.5 g protein, 96.5 g carbohydrate, 55 mg cholesterol, 245 mg sodium, 3 g fiber

Orange-Almond Cake with Citrus Glaze

Intense, fresh orange flavor permeates this delightful cake. Its moist texture is punctuated by a slight crunch from the ground almonds. In addition to a fine ending to an evening meal, it makes a lovely addition to a brunch menu.

CAKE
- 1¼ cups slivered almonds
- 1½ cups sugar, divided
- 1¼ cups all-purpose flour
- 2½ teaspoons baking powder
- ¾ teaspoon salt
- 3 eggs, separated
- ⅛ teaspoon cream of tartar
- 2 eggs
- ½ cup extra-light olive oil
- 1½ tablespoons grated orange peel
- 1 teaspoon grated lemon peel
- 1 teaspoon orange extract
- ½ teaspoon almond extract
- ¾ cup orange juice with pulp

GLAZE
- 1½ cups powdered sugar
- 1 to 2 tablespoons orange juice
- 1 teaspoon lemon juice
- 2 teaspoons grated orange peel

1 Heat oven to 350°F. Grease 10-inch nonstick Bundt pan with shortening. Sprinkle with flour; tap sides of pan to remove excess.
2 In food processor, combine almonds and ¼ cup of the sugar;

Orange-Almond Cake with Citrus Glaze

pulse 1 minute or until almonds are very finely ground. Place in medium bowl; whisk in flour, baking powder and salt.

3 Place 3 egg whites and cream of tartar in large bowl; reserve yolks. Beat at medium-high speed 30 seconds or until foamy. With mixer running, slowly add 3/4 cup of the sugar; beat 3 to 4 minutes or until soft peaks form. Place in small bowl.

4 In same large bowl, beat 2 eggs, reserved 3 egg yolks, olive oil, remaining 1/2 cup sugar, 1 1/2 tablespoons orange peel, lemon peel, orange extract and almond extract at medium speed 2 minutes or until pale yellow. Slowly add orange juice; beat 1 minute.

5 Whisk in flour mixture. Add 1 cup of the egg whites; gently whisk to lighten mixture. Fold in remaining egg whites. Pour into pan. Bake 35 to 40 minutes or until golden brown and toothpick inserted in center comes out clean. Cool cake in pan on wire rack 10 minutes. Invert onto wire rack; cool completely.

6 Meanwhile, in medium bowl, whisk powdered sugar, 1 tablespoon of the orange juice and lemon juice until smooth, adding additional orange juice if necessary. Stir in 2 teaspoons orange peel. Drizzle glaze over cake.

12 servings

PER SERVING: 400 calories, 18 g total fat (2.5 g saturated fat), 6.5 g protein, 55.5 g carbohydrate, 90 mg cholesterol, 295 mg sodium, 2 g fiber

Golden Zucchini Cake with Apricots and Raisins

This variation on the ever-popular zucchini cake calls on apricots and raisins for interesting taste and texture. You can substitute a mild olive oil or even a nonassertive extra-virgin olive oil for the extra-light oil. The spices will stand up to the stronger flavors.

CAKE
1 1/2 cups all-purpose flour
1/2 teaspoon baking soda
1/2 teaspoon salt

Olive Oil for Baking

Choosing For mildly flavored cakes, use a cold-pressed olive oil that is graded extra-light (also called extra-light tasting). Bertolli, Filippo Berrio and Carapelli are three imported Italian brands that are widely available. Extra-light is ideal for baking because it's bland-tasting and free of aroma. It can be used as an all-purpose substitute for other vegetable oils in all baking and cooking.

A delicately flavored olive oil can be used with stronger flavored cakes, such as spice, chocolate or pumpkin. The slightly perfumed Bertolli Classico is a good choice.

Cold pressed extra-virgin oil, with its more robust olive taste and aroma, is not recommended for cakes.

Storing Always smell and taste olive oil before deciding whether to use it. Oils are volatile and can lose their flavors and go rancid when exposed too long to heat, moisture, air or light. Rancid fat not only spoils the taste of baked goods, but it is unhealthy to ingest. Store olive oil in an opaque container in a cool, dark place. You also can refrigerate it if you wish. The oil may become cloudy when it's cold, but it will clarify as it warms to room temperature.

Comparing Fat All oils are 100 percent fat, and all oils contain 14 grams of fat and 120 calories per tablespoon. But olive oil delivers a bonus: It contains more monounsaturated fat (77 percent) than any other fat or oil. In many studies, monounsaturated fat has been shown to lower the levels of LDLs (low-density lipoproteins, the bad fats) in blood serum cholesterol without decreasing the levels of high-density lipoproteins (HDLs, the good fats). In contrast, canola oil contains 62 percent monounsaturated fat, peanut oil has 49 percent, butter has 30 percent, corn oil has 25 percent and safflower oil has 13 percent.

1 teaspoon ground cinnamon
1/2 teaspoon ground nutmeg
1/4 teaspoon ground ginger
1/4 teaspoon baking powder
1/3 cup finely diced dried apricots
1/3 cup golden raisins
2 eggs, room temperature
1 cup sugar
1/2 cup extra-light olive oil
1 1/2 teaspoons vanilla
1 cup lightly packed shredded zucchini
FROSTING
4 oz. cream cheese, softened
1/4 cup unsalted butter, softened
Dash salt
2 cups powdered sugar
1 teaspoon vanilla

1 Heat oven to 350°F. Spray 8x8x2-inch pan with nonstick cooking spray. Sprinkle with flour; tap sides of pan to remove excess.

2 In medium bowl, whisk together flour, baking soda, 1/2 teaspoon salt, cinnamon, nutmeg, ginger and baking powder. In small bowl, stir together apricots, raisins and 1/4 cup of the flour mixture until fruit is well coated.

3 In large bowl, beat eggs, sugar, olive oil and 1 1/2 teaspoons vanilla at medium speed until blended. At low speed, slowly beat in flour mixture until blended; stir in apricot mixture and zucchini. Pour batter into pan; bake 45 to 50 minutes or until toothpick inserted in center comes out with just a few crumbs attached. Cool completely in pan on wire rack.

4 Meanwhile, in medium bowl, beat cream cheese, butter and salt at medium speed until blended and smooth. Add powdered sugar and 1 teaspoon vanilla; beat until smooth and creamy.

5 Spread frosting over cooled cake. Refrigerate leftovers.

12 servings

PER SERVING: 385 calories, 17 g total fat (6 g saturated fat), 4 g protein, 55 g carbohydrate, 55 mg cholesterol, 225 mg sodium, 1 g fiber

Chocolate-Buttermilk Cake with Apricot Preserves

Buttermilk gives this rich cake an especially tender crumb; brown sugar and olive oil add moisture and enhance its keeping quality. In fact, the cake actually tastes better the second day. The batter is very thin, but don't worry — the cake rises nicely and is dense and moist.

CAKE
1¾ cups all-purpose flour
¾ cup Dutch-process cocoa
1¼ teaspoons baking powder
½ teaspoon baking soda
¾ teaspoon salt
3 eggs, room temperature
2 cups packed dark brown
   sugar
1 cup buttermilk
½ cup warm water
½ cup extra-light olive oil
2 teaspoons vanilla

FROSTING
4 oz. semisweet chocolate,
   chopped
¼ cup unsalted butter, cut up,
   softened
2½ cups powdered sugar
   Dash salt
1 teaspoon vanilla
4 to 5 tablespoons milk

FILLING
¾ cup apricot preserves

1 Heat oven to 350°F. Spray 2 (9x1½-inch) round cake pans with nonstick cooking spray. Line bottoms of pans with parchment. Spray

Better Blending

To ensure the cocoa, flour and other dry ingredients in *Chocolate-Buttermilk Cake* (left) are well-blended, use a wire whisk to mix them instead of a spoon.

parchment with nonstick cooking spray; sprinkle with unsweetened cocoa. Tap sides of pans to remove excess.

2 In medium bowl, whisk together flour, cocoa, baking powder, baking soda and salt to blend. In large bowl, beat eggs, brown sugar, buttermilk, water, oil and 2 teaspoons vanilla at medium speed until well blended. Sift flour mixture over buttermilk mixture. Beat at low speed 1 minute or until well blended, occasionally scraping down sides of bowl.

3 Pour batter evenly into pans. Bake 30 to 35 minutes or until toothpick inserted in center comes out clean. Cool in pans on wire rack 20 minutes. Invert onto wire rack; remove parchment. Cool completely.

4 Meanwhile, in medium saucepan, combine chocolate and butter. Heat over low heat until melted and smooth, stirring frequently. Pour into

large bowl; cool 5 minutes. Sift powdered sugar and salt over chocolate mixture; beat at low speed until blended. Beat in 1 teaspoon vanilla and 4 tablespoons milk at low speed until blended. Increase speed to medium-high; beat 1 to 2 minutes or until creamy, adding additional milk if frosting is too thick.

5 Place one cake layer on serving platter or cardboard round; top with apricot preserves, spreading to within ¼ inch of edge. Top with second cake layer. Spread cake sides with thin layer of frosting. Coat sides with another layer of frosting; spread remaining frosting on top.

12 servings

PER SERVING: 555 calories, 18.5 g total fat (6.5 g saturated fat), 6 g protein, 97.5 g carbohydrate, 65 mg cholesterol, 335 mg sodium, 3 g fiber

Susan G. Purdy is the author of *The Perfect Cake* (Broadway Books).

Chocolate-Buttermilk Cake with Apricot Preserves

Fresh Cranberry-Studded Bread Pudding

Fall for Desserts

Cozy up to these heartwarming dishes featuring autumn's classic fruits.

Recipes by Carolyn Weil

The fruits of fall inspire all manner of homey indulgences. Pies, tarts and crisps are the classic venues for apples, pears and cranberries. And we find perfect cheer in every bite.

The addition of sweet spices and crunchy nuts only heightens our pleasure, turning what is merely delicious into downright divine. Apples and cardamom, almonds and pears, cranberries and cinnamon. Who can resist these pairings? If the aromas don't grab you, the tastes certainly will.

Fresh Cranberry-Studded Bread Pudding

Use firm, dense white bread for this pudding. While fresh bread will work, day-old or slightly stale bread is preferable because it adds texture and contrast to the custard.

CRANBERRIES
- 1 cup sugar
- ³⁄₄ cup water
- 2¹⁄₂ cups fresh cranberries or frozen cranberries, thawed

BREAD PUDDING
- 3 cups toasted cubed (1 inch) bread (crusts removed)
- 3 eggs
- 2 egg yolks
- ³⁄₄ cup sugar
- 1 teaspoon vanilla extract
- ¹⁄₂ teaspoon ground cinnamon
- ¹⁄₄ teaspoon ground nutmeg
- ¹⁄₄ teaspoon ground cloves
- ¹⁄₄ teaspoon salt
- 1¹⁄₂ cups whipping cream

CREAM
- 1 cup whipping cream
- 1 tablespoon sugar

1 In medium saucepan, bring 1 cup sugar and water to a boil over medium-high heat. Reduce heat to medium; boil 5 minutes. Add cranberries; cook 5 minutes or until all cranberries have popped and mixture is thickened. Place in medium bowl; refrigerate 30 minutes or until warm but not hot.

2 Heat oven to 325°F. Place bread in 11¹⁄₂x8-inch (2-quart) glass baking dish. Spoon cranberries over bread.

3 In medium bowl, whisk together eggs, egg yolks and ³⁄₄ cup sugar until blended. Whisk in vanilla, cinnamon, nutmeg, cloves and salt. Stir in 1¹⁄₂ cups cream. Pour mixture over bread. Place baking dish in large shallow pan; add enough hot tap water to come halfway up sides of baking dish. Bake in water bath 50 to 55 minutes or until custard is golden and slightly puffed in center. Remove from water bath; cool on wire rack 15 to 20 minutes.

4 In medium bowl, beat cream ingredients at medium-high speed until stiff peaks form. Serve with warm bread pudding.

8 servings

PER SERVING: 490 calories, 27 g total fat (15.5 g saturated fat), 6 g protein, 58.5 g carbohydrate, 215 mg cholesterol, 195 mg sodium, 1.5 g fiber

Apple-Cardamom Upside-Down Cake

This cake is best enjoyed warm from the oven. If you wish, serve it with a scoop of vanilla bean ice cream sprinkled with a little cardamom. If the apples don't look perfectly positioned when you invert the cake, simply rearrange them with a fork while the cake is still warm.

TOPPING
- ¹⁄₃ cup unsalted butter
- 1 cup packed brown sugar
- 3 medium apples (Braeburn, Pippin or Jonagold), peeled, sliced (¹⁄₂ inch) (about 3³⁄₄ cups)
- ¹⁄₂ cup chopped walnuts

CAKE
- 1¹⁄₂ cups all-purpose flour
- 1¹⁄₂ teaspoons ground cardamom
- 1 teaspoon baking powder
- ¹⁄₂ teaspoon salt
- ¹⁄₂ cup unsalted butter, softened
- 1 cup sugar
- 2 eggs, room temperature
- ¹⁄₂ cup milk

1 Heat oven to 350°F. Spray 10-inch round cake pan with nonstick cooking spray. Line bottom with parchment paper. Melt ¹⁄₃ cup butter in medium skillet over medium heat. Stir in brown sugar; cook 2 to 3 minutes or until bubbly, stirring occasionally. Spread in cake pan. Arrange apple slices over brown sugar mixture. Sprinkle with walnuts.

2 In medium bowl, stir together flour, cardamom, baking powder and salt. In large bowl, beat ¹⁄₂ cup butter at medium speed until fluffy. Add sugar; beat until mixture is pale yellow. Add eggs one at a time, beating well after each addition. At low speed, beat in flour mixture

alternately with milk, beginning and ending with flour mixture. Spread over apples.

3 Bake 45 to 50 minutes or until cake is golden brown, center is firm to touch, and toothpick inserted in center comes out clean. Cool on wire rack 5 minutes. Invert onto serving plate; remove parchment paper. Rearrange apples if necessary. Cool an additional 15 to 20 minutes; serve warm.

8 servings

PER SERVING: 555 calories, 25.5 g total fat (13 g saturated fat), 6 g protein, 79.5 g carbohydrate, 105 mg cholesterol, 245 mg sodium, 2 g fiber

Pear Crisp with Candied Ginger and Five-Spice Powder

Candied ginger and Chinese five-spice powder jazz up this homey dish. Serve it soon after baking, with whipped cream or vanilla ice cream.

TOPPING
- 1 cup old-fashioned rolled oats
- ½ cup all-purpose flour
- ½ cup packed brown sugar
- ¼ teaspoon five-spice powder*
- ¼ teaspoon salt
- ½ cup finely chopped walnuts
- ¼ cup chopped crystallized ginger
- ½ cup unsalted butter, chilled, cut up

FILLING
- ½ cup sugar
- ¼ teaspoon five-spice powder
- 1 tablespoon cornstarch
  Dash salt
- 6 cups peeled chopped (½ inch) Anjou pears (about 6 pears)

1 In medium bowl, stir together all topping ingredients except butter. With pastry blender or 2 knives, cut butter into flour mixture until mixture is crumbly. Refrigerate while making filling.

2 Heat oven to 350°F. In large bowl, stir together all filling ingredients except pears. Add pears; toss until pears are well-coated.

3 Spoon into 11½x8-inch (2-quart) baking dish; sprinkle evenly with topping. Bake 45 to 50 minutes or until topping is crisp and golden brown and fruit bubbles slowly around edges. Serve warm.

TIP *Five-spice powder is a prepared seasoning that often includes star anise, cloves, cinnamon, fennel seed and pepper. It can be found in the spice or Asian foods section of the grocery store.

8 servings

PER SERVING: 410 calories, 17.5 g total fat (7.5 g saturated fat), 4 g protein, 64 g carbohydrate, 30 mg cholesterol, 130 mg sodium, 5 g fiber

Almond Frangipane Tart with Pears and Cranberries

Frangipane is a thick pastry cream made with almonds. It imparts a delicious flavor and prevents the bottom crust from getting soggy from the fruit filling. The tip on page 131 shows you how to fan pear slices on top for a beautiful presentation.

DOUGH
- 1½ cups all-purpose flour
- ¼ cup sugar
- ¼ teaspoon salt
- ½ cup unsalted butter, chilled, cut up
- ¼ cup cold water

FILLING
- 1½ cups (8 oz.) whole blanched almonds
- ⅔ cup sugar, divided
- 2 eggs
- 2 tablespoons dark rum or orange juice
- 1 teaspoon vanilla extract
- ½ teaspoon almond extract
- 1 teaspoon grated lemon peel
- ¼ teaspoon salt
- 2 tablespoons unsalted butter, melted
- 2 ripe but firm small Anjou pears, peeled, quartered
- 27 fresh cranberries

GLAZE
- 2 tablespoons apricot preserves

1 In medium bowl, stir together flour, ¼ cup sugar and ¼ teaspoon salt. With pastry blender or 2 knives, cut chilled butter into flour mixture until mixture resembles coarse crumbs with some pea-sized pieces. Sprinkle water evenly over mixture; stir until dough forms.

2 Shape dough into small flat round. On lightly floured surface, roll into 12-inch round. Place dough in bottom and up sides of 9½-inch tart pan with removable bottom; trim edges by pressing rolling pin across top of pan. Refrigerate 15 to 20 minutes or until cool.

3 Meanwhile, heat oven to 375°F. Line tart crust with foil; fill with pie weights or dried beans. Bake 18 to 20 minutes or until edges are light golden brown. Remove from oven; remove foil and pie weights. If center looks wet, bake an additional 2 to 4 minutes. Cool on wire rack while preparing filling.

4 In food processor, pulse almonds with ⅓ cup of the sugar until finely ground. In medium bowl, whisk together remaining ⅓ cup sugar, eggs, rum, vanilla, almond extract, lemon peel, ¼ teaspoon salt and melted butter. Stir in ground almond mixture. Place tart pan on baking sheet. Spread filling in crust.

5 Slice quartered pears crosswise into thin slices. Press sliced pear quarters slightly to fan before placing them on filling. Place 3 cranberries in center of tart and between each pear section. Lightly press into filling. Bake tart on baking sheet 45 to 50 minutes or until filling is firm in center and golden brown around edges. Place tart on wire rack.

6 In small saucepan, warm preserves over low heat until melted; brush over pears. Cool 20 to 30 minutes. Serve tart warm.

8 servings

PER SERVING: 455 calories, 27 g total fat (8.5 g saturated fat), 9 g protein, 46.5 g carbohydrate, 80 mg cholesterol, 145 mg sodium, 4.5 g fiber

Almond Frangipane Tart with
Pears and Cranberries

Maple, Apple and Pear Pie

Maple, Apple and Pear Pie

The combination of apples, pears and maple syrup makes a filling that is light in texture, full of fruit flavors and not too sweet. Use grade B maple syrup, if possible, for a deep maple flavor.

DOUGH
- 2¼ cups all-purpose flour
- 6 tablespoons sugar
- ¼ teaspoon salt
- ¾ cup unsalted butter, chilled, cut up
- 6 tablespoons cold water

FILLING
- 3 cups sliced (¼ inch) peeled Braeburn or Fuji apples (about 3 medium)
- 3 cups sliced (¼ inch) peeled Anjou pears (about 3 medium)
- 2½ tablespoons cornstarch
- Dash salt
- ⅔ cup grade B pure maple syrup*
- 1 tablespoon unsalted butter
- 1 tablespoon sugar

1 In large bowl, stir together flour, sugar and ¼ teaspoon salt. With pastry blender or 2 knives, cut chilled butter into flour mixture until mixture resembles coarse crumbs with some pea-sized pieces. Sprinkle water evenly over mixture; stir until dough forms. Divide dough in half; shape each piece into small flat round. Refrigerate 30 minutes or until firm.

2 In large bowl, toss together apples, pears, cornstarch and dash salt. Drizzle with maple syrup; stir gently to combine.

3 On lightly floured surface, roll 1 dough half into 12-inch round about ⅛ inch thick. Place in 9-inch pie plate; trim edges even with outside rim.

4 Spoon fruit mixture into crust; dot with 1 tablespoon butter. On lightly floured surface, roll remaining dough half into 12-inch round; place over fruit. Trim edge to 1-inch overhang. Fold over bottom crust edge; flute edges. Sprinkle 1 tablespoon sugar

over crust. Cut several steam slits in top crust. Refrigerate 15 minutes.

5 Meanwhile, place oven rack in lower third of oven. Heat oven to 375°F. Bake 15 minutes. Reduce oven temperature to 350°F.; bake an additional 55 to 65 minutes or until crust is golden brown and fruit is tender when pierced with knife. Cover edge of pie crust with foil during last 15 minutes if browning too quickly. Cool on wire rack 30 to 40 minutes; serve slightly warm.

Fanning Pear Slices

Pears fanned across the top of *Almond Frangipane Tart* (page 128) make a beautiful presentation. To achieve this look, peel the pears and cut into quarters; remove the core. Cut each quarter crosswise into thin slices while keeping the quarter shape intact. Lightly press the sliced quarters to fan the slices. Use a metal spatula to transfer the slices to the tart. Lightly press them into the filling.

TIP *Look for grade B maple syrup in food co-ops. It has a very dark color and rich flavor. If unavailable, use the more common grade A.

8 servings

PER SERVING: 475 calories, 19.5 g total fat (11.5 g saturated fat), 4 g protein, 73.5 g carbohydrate, 50 mg cholesterol, 115 mg sodium, 3 g fiber

Carolyn Weil is a frequent contributor to Cooking Pleasures.

Caramel-Pecan Cupcakes

Grown-Up Cupcakes

Sophisticated flavors star in these adult versions of a childhood favorite.

Text and Recipes by Lisa Saltzman

For years cupcakes have been the ultimate treat at children's parties. But children aren't the only ones whose eyes light up when a platter of cupcakes is brought into a room. There are plenty of adults who secretly look forward to kids' celebrations so that they, too, can indulge in this pleasure.

Now imagine how delightful it would be if those cupcakes had grown-up flavors — fresh lime and toasted coconut, Grand Marnier, chocolate fudge and caramel pecan. Add sophisticated presentations, and they're transformed into elegant pastries in a miniature version. The next time you entertain, indulge your guests with a dessert that plays to the child within.

Caramel-Pecan Cupcakes

Toasting the pecans in the oven brings out a wonderful nuttiness that enhances the aroma and flavor of these cupcakes.

CUPCAKES
- 1¼ cups coarsely chopped toasted pecans, divided*
- 1 cup sugar, divided
- ½ cup unsalted butter, softened
- 2 eggs
- 1 teaspoon vanilla
- 1½ cups sifted all-purpose flour
- ½ teaspoon baking powder
- ½ teaspoon baking soda
- ½ teaspoon salt
- ⅓ cup sour cream

FROSTING
- 3 egg yolks
- 6 tablespoons sugar
- 4 tablespoons water, divided
- ½ cup unsalted butter, cut up, softened
- ½ teaspoon vanilla

1 Heat oven to 350°F. Grease 12-cup muffin pan or line with baking cups.

2 Place 1 cup of the pecans and ¼ cup of the sugar in food processor. Pulse until finely ground and fluffy, being careful not to make paste.

3 In large bowl, beat remaining ¾ cup sugar and ½ cup butter at medium speed 5 to 6 minutes or until light and fluffy. Add eggs one at a time, beating well after each addition. Beat in 1 teaspoon vanilla.

4 In medium bowl, stir together flour, baking powder, baking soda, salt and 1 cup ground pecans. At low speed, beat sour cream into sugar mixture alternately with flour mixture. Spoon into muffin cups, filling two-thirds full. Bake 25 to 30 minutes or until golden brown and toothpick inserted in center comes out clean. Cool on wire rack 10 minutes. Remove from pan; cool completely.

5 To make frosting, in large bowl, beat egg yolks at medium-high speed 5 minutes or until light, fluffy and pale colored.

6 Meanwhile, in small saucepan, combine 6 tablespoons sugar and 1 tablespoon of the water. Cook over medium-high heat, without stirring, 4 to 6 minutes or until sugar turns golden amber color. Remove from heat; carefully add remaining 3 tablespoons water. Return to heat; cook, stirring, until sugar is dissolved.

7 Slowly add sugar mixture to beaten egg yolks, beating at medium-high speed 5 minutes or until mixture has cooled. Add ½ cup butter a few pieces at a time; add ½ teaspoon vanilla. Beat until smooth.

8 Spread each cupcake with thick layer of frosting. Very finely chop remaining ¼ cup pecans; roll edges of cupcakes in nuts.

TIP *To toast pecans, spread on baking sheet; bake at 375°F. for 7 to 10 minutes or until light golden brown.

12 cupcakes

PER CUPCAKE: 405 calories, 27 g total fat (11.5 g saturated fat), 4.5 g protein, 37.5 g carbohydrate, 135 mg cholesterol, 185 mg sodium, 1.5 g fiber

Coconut-Lime Cupcakes

These wonderfully moist cakes are loaded with lime flavor. They would make a lovely addition to an Asian menu, a tropical grilled meal or a brunch spread.

CUPCAKES
- 6 tablespoons unsalted butter, softened
- ¾ cup sugar
- 1 egg
- 1 tablespoon finely grated lime peel
- 1 teaspoon fresh lime juice
- 1½ cups all-purpose flour
- ½ teaspoon baking powder
- ½ teaspoon baking soda
- ½ teaspoon salt
- 1 cup sour cream

FROSTING
- 1 cup whipping cream
- ¼ cup powdered sugar
- 1 teaspoon lime juice
- 1 teaspoon grated lime peel

GARNISH
- 1 cup finely shredded coconut

1 Heat oven to 350°F. Grease 12-cup muffin pan or line with baking cups.

In large bowl, beat butter and sugar at medium speed 5 to 6 minutes or until light and fluffy. Beat in egg, 1 tablespoon lime peel and 1 teaspoon lime juice.

2 In medium bowl, stir together flour, baking powder, baking soda and salt. At low speed, beat sour cream into butter mixture alternately with flour mixture. Spoon batter into muffin pan, filling two-thirds full. Bake 25 to 30 minutes or until golden brown and toothpick inserted in center comes out clean. Cool on wire rack 10 minutes. Remove from pan; cool completely.

3 In large bowl, beat all frosting ingredients at medium speed until stiff peaks form. Spread each cupcake with frosting; sprinkle with coconut. Refrigerate until ready to serve.

12 servings

PER CUPCAKE: 320 calories, 21 g total fat (14.5 g saturated fat), 3.5 g protein, 30.5 g carbohydrate, 70 mg cholesterol, 195 mg sodium, 1.5 g fiber

Coconut-Lime Cupcakes

Easier Cupcakes

You can avoid the mess of filling muffin pans and baking cups with these helpful hints.

- If you bake cupcakes directly in the muffin pans, grease the cups with nonstick cooking spray. If you use foil baking cups, grease these too. This helps the liner release without damaging the cupcake. On the other hand, if you use paper baking cups, do not grease them because the spray tends to flatten the papers.

- To fill the muffin pans or cups neatly, use a homemade piping bag. Place a large, heavy-duty, resealable plastic bag in a quart container. Fold down the top. Spoon the prepared batter into the bag, press out any excess air and seal the bag. Make a 1-inch cut across one corner and squeeze the batter into the cups, filling each two-thirds full.

- You can freeze unbaked cupcake batter for future use. Make the batter and fill the cups as usual, using baking cups. Place the whole pan in the freezer for several hours until the batter has frozen. Remove the individual cupcakes from the pan and store them in a plastic freezer bag or airtight container. When you're ready to bake them, place the frozen cupcakes in a muffin pan and bake according to the original recipe, adding another 5 to 10 minutes baking time, or until they're set and a toothpick inserted in the center comes out clean.

Grand Marnier Cupcakes

Grand Marnier Cupcakes

The chocolate garnish on these luscious cupcakes marries well with the Grand Marnier. If chocolate is your passion, serve the cupcakes with a pitcher of dark chocolate sauce on the side.

CUPCAKES
- 6 tablespoons unsalted butter, softened
- ¾ cup sugar
- 1 egg
- 1 tablespoon finely grated orange peel
- 1 teaspoon Grand Marnier or orange juice
- 1½ cups all-purpose flour
- ½ teaspoon baking powder
- ½ teaspoon baking soda
- ½ teaspoon salt
- 1 cup sour cream

GLAZE
- ⅓ cup sugar
- 2 tablespoons fresh orange juice
- 2 tablespoons Grand Marnier or additional orange juice

TOPPING
- 3 oz. semisweet chocolate, coarsely chopped
- ½ teaspoon shortening

1 Heat oven to 350°F. Grease 12-cup muffin pan or line with baking cups. In large bowl, beat butter and ¾ cup sugar at medium speed 5 to 6 minutes or until light and fluffy. Beat in egg, 1 tablespoon orange peel and 1 teaspoon Grand Marnier.

2 In medium bowl, stir together flour, baking powder, baking soda and salt. At low speed, beat sour cream into butter mixture alternately with flour mixture. Spoon batter into muffin pan, filling two-thirds full.

3 Bake 20 to 25 minutes or until golden brown and toothpick inserted in center comes out clean. Cool on wire rack 10 minutes. Remove from pan; cool completely.

4 Meanwhile, in small saucepan, heat ⅓ cup sugar and orange juice over medium heat until sugar dissolves. Remove from heat; stir in 2 tablespoons Grand Marnier.

5 Poke holes with toothpick in top of each cupcake. Using pastry brush, brush tops liberally with Grand Marnier glaze.

6 Place chocolate in small heavy resealable plastic bag; add shortening and seal. Place in pan of simmering water; turn off heat. Allow bag to sit several minutes; remove from water. Smooth melted chocolate by working bag with hands. Cool 5 minutes. Cut off tiny corner of bag; drizzle chocolate over cupcakes.

12 cupcakes

PER CUPCAKE: 265 calories, 12.5 g total fat (7.5 g saturated fat), 3 g protein, 36.5 g carbohydrate, 45 mg cholesterol, 185 mg sodium, 1 g fiber

Chocolate Fudge Cupcakes

These cupcakes are a chocolate-lover's dream. Their fudgy flavor is complemented by a light, delicate texture, similar to that of a sponge cake. Topped with a melt-in-your-mouth frosting and chocolate curls, they're irresistible.

CUPCAKES
¾ cup unsalted butter
6 oz. semisweet chocolate, chopped
¾ cup sugar
4 eggs, separated
½ cup all-purpose flour
¾ teaspoon baking powder
½ teaspoon cream of tartar

FROSTING AND GARNISH
12 oz. semisweet chocolate, coarsely chopped, divided
3 tablespoons whipping cream

1 Heat oven to 325°F. Grease 12-cup muffin pan or line with baking cups. Place metal bowl over medium saucepan of barely simmering water (bowl should not touch water). Add

Chocolate Fudge Cupcakes

butter and 6 oz. chocolate. Let stand until melted; stir until smooth. Cool to room temperature. Whisk in sugar and egg yolks. Stir in flour and baking powder.

2 In large bowl, beat egg whites at medium speed until frothy. Add cream of tartar. Beat at medium-high speed until soft peaks form. Fold one-fourth of the whites into chocolate mixture. Gently fold in remaining whites until mixed.

3 Spoon batter into muffin cups, filling two-thirds full. Bake 25 to 30 minutes or until toothpick inserted in center comes out clean. Cool on wire rack 10 minutes. Remove from pan; cool completely.

4 To make chocolate curls for garnish, line 4x2½-inch mini loaf pan with plastic wrap. Melt 6 oz. of the chocolate in metal bowl set over pan of barely simmering water (do not let bowl touch water). Pour into mini loaf pan; cool until firm. Unmold chocolate; remove plastic wrap. Using vegetable peeler, make curls.

5 In medium saucepan, combine remaining 6 oz. semisweet chocolate and whipping cream. Heat over low heat until melted and smooth, stirring frequently. Spread each cupcake with frosting; let cupcakes stand until frosting is cool but not set. Garnish with chocolate curls.

12 cupcakes

PER CUPCAKE: 410 calories, 27 g total fat (16 g saturated fat), 4.5 g protein, 44 g carbohydrate, 105 mg cholesterol, 60 mg sodium, 2.5 g fiber

Lisa Saltzman is a cooking school instructor and a former pastry chef living in Eugene, Oregon.

Chocolate Curls

The chocolate curls that garnish *Chocolate Fudge Cupcakes* (page 136) are easiest to make if you use a large block of chocolate. To make a block, melt the chocolate and pour it into a mini loaf pan lined with plastic wrap. Or make your own pan by forming a double thickness of foil into a rectangular shape. Once the block has cooled and hardened, you can make the curls. Hold the block in one hand with plastic wrap to minimize melting. Draw a vegetable peeler across the length of the block. For best results, the block should be slightly soft. If the block is too hard (producing flakes rather than curls), soften it slightly by microwaving it on the defrost setting for 5 to 10 seconds.

Razzberry Truffles

Fearless Chocolate

Tame your fears about tempering chocolate with this amazingly easy method.

Text and Recipes by Elaine González

When love is in the air (and even when it isn't), thoughts often turn to chocolate. There's no other food that symbolizes affection like chocolate candy. It's even better when you make it yourself.

Unfortunately, many people never attempt chocolate-making at home. That's because to produce professional-quality truffles, fancy molded pieces and other delectable chocolate confections, the process requires the chocolate to be tempered. And because most candy-making instructions make the tempering process sound complicated, many home cooks give up without even trying.

If you've left chocolate-making to the pros, take heart. There is a way to temper chocolate that's fast and easy and ensures success. If you have a microwave and some inexpensive tools, you can produce chocolates that rival fine commercial products. Once you learn the technique, you'll wonder why you ever hesitated. Homemade chocolates are the perfect gift of love — to your friends, your family or even yourself.

Razzberry Truffles

Lemon juice adds a little zing to these flavorful raspberry truffles and extends their shelf life when stored in a cool place. The cornstarch makes the mixture easier to roll into balls and forms a thin, flavorless crust, enabling you to dip them at room temperature. It's not necessary to temper the chocolate that's used to make the truffle centers. For professional results, however, truffle centers should be dipped in tempered chocolate. It is thicker than untempered chocolate, clings better and is less likely to form a puddle at the bottom of the truffle. Best of all, the truffles will remain shiny — even at room temperature.

CENTERS
- 8 oz. semisweet chocolate, coarsely chopped
- ¼ cup unsalted butter
- 2 tablespoons heavy whipping cream
- ½ cup raspberry jam
- 2 tablespoons lemon juice
- ½ cup cornstarch

SHELL
- 1½ lb. semisweet chocolate, coarsely chopped,
- 6 oz. semisweet chocolate, in 1 or 2 pieces

- ¼ cup unsweetened cocoa
- ¼ cup finely chopped roasted hazelnuts

1 To make centers, melt 8 oz. chocolate.

2 Meanwhile, heat butter and cream in small saucepan over medium heat until butter is melted and small bubbles form around edges. Pour into medium bowl. Stir in melted chocolate. Whisk in jam and lemon juice, blending until smooth. Cover loosely; refrigerate 1 to 1½ hours or until firm.

3 Line baking sheet with parchment or waxed paper. Spoon truffle mixture into mounds on parchment paper; use about 2 teaspoons per truffle to make 36 truffle centers. Refrigerate 15 minutes or until firm.

4 Dust hands with cornstarch and roll mounds into balls, coating hands with cornstarch as needed. Arrange on another lined baking sheet. Let stand, uncovered, at room temperature at least 2 hours or overnight until thin crust forms.

5 Line another baking sheet with parchment or waxed paper. For shell, melt 1½ lb. chocolate in medium bowl. Stir until smooth. Temper using 6 oz. chocolate.

6 Place bowl of tempered chocolate on folded towel doubled in back so bowl tilts slightly forward. Place truffle centers on one side of bowl and lined baking sheet on the other.

7 Immerse truffle center in chocolate, rounded side up.* Using dipping fork or regular fork, remove truffle from chocolate. Tap fork several times to drain excess chocolate; lightly scrape fork on rim of bowl. Place truffle on lined baking sheet using toothpick or skewer to slide it off fork. Repeat with remaining truffle centers.

8 Sift cocoa powder over tops of dipped truffles or sprinkle with nuts before chocolate dries. Refrigerate 10 minutes or until set.

TIP *For best shine, dip truffles in cool room, about 65°F. to 70°F. If room is warm, dip and refrigerate 12 centers at a time. Centers should be at room temperature when dipped. A cold dipped center will expand when it warms to room temperature, causing chocolate shell to crack and filling to ooze out.

36 truffles

PER TRUFFLE: 100 calories, 6.5 g total fat (3.5 g saturated fat), 1 g protein, 2 g carbohydrate, 5 mg cholesterol, 5 mg sodium, 1 g fiber

Tempering Chocolate

Chocolate is usually "in temper" when you buy it: Its surface is glossy and unblemished, it snaps when you break it, and its interior is smooth and uniform in color. Heating it melts the cocoa butter, and the chocolate becomes smooth and creamy. As it cools, the liquid cocoa butter crystallizes, causing the chocolate to solidify.

A similar thing happens when you freeze water. Ice crystals begin to grow and the water solidifies. But unlike ice crystals, which only grow in one form, cocoa butter crystallizes in two forms — stable (good) and unstable (bad). The goal of tempering is to maintain the good crystals and eliminate the bad ones. This is done by gently heating, stirring and cooling the chocolate to a certain range of temperatures.

Melted chocolate must be tempered to make candy, chocolate decorations and dipped fruit or nuts. Tempered chocolate sets quickly, releases from molds easily and holds its shape when you pipe designs with it. Untempered chocolate does just the opposite: It sets slowly, sticks to molds and dries with a dull, streaked surface (called bloom). It is not necessary to temper chocolate when it is used for baking.

The Easiest Method

There's more than one way to temper chocolate, but one of the easiest methods is to drop one or two glossy, unblemished chunks of chocolate into a bowl of melted chocolate and stir them gently to cool the chocolate. The chunks, which contain stable cocoa butter crystals, partially melt and "seed" the bowl with good crystals, thereby tempering the chocolate.

A chocolate chopper is a very effective tool for chopping chocolate. A heavy serrated knife also can be used.

After melting the chocolate, add the chunk of chocolate to start the tempering process.

Gently stir the melted chocolate and the chunk, monitoring the temperature.

When the chocolate has reached 90°F., remove the partially melted chunk.

Test the temper by smearing a chocolate sample on waxed paper. It's ready when it's firm, evenly glossy and snaps when you break it. The smear at the top of the photo is not in temper.

Melting the Chocolate To begin the process, you first must melt the chocolate. Use a chocolate chopper or a heavy serrated knife to chop the chocolate into almond-sized pieces. It will melt faster and more easily. The chunks used to temper the chocolate should be kept large so they are easy to retrieve when the correct temperature is achieved. The microwave does a quick and efficient job of melting large and small amounts of chocolate. Use a microwave-safe plastic bowl because it stays cooler than glass or ceramic. Because all microwaves differ, use the suggested time increments in the recipe (below) as a guide and adjust them to suit your oven. You also can melt chocolate in a heatproof bowl over hot water — not steaming, simmering or boiling water. Stir occasionally with a rubber spatula as it melts. Once it's melted, lift the bowl out of the pan and dry the bottom.

If the chocolate to be melted appears dull, blemished or grainy, it must be heated to specific temperatures to melt the bad crystals it contains: dark chocolate (semisweet and bittersweet) to 115°F., and milk and white chocolates to 110°F. Let the chocolate cool to 100°F. before proceeding. Stir the chocolate frequently as it melts, using a flexible rubber spatula; this is especially important when using the microwave. When a recipe calls for melting chocolate chips, substitute an equal amount of chocolate in bar form. Most bars of chocolate contain more cocoa butter than chocolate chips and will melt more fluidly.

Adding the Chunks The chunks that are added to temper the chocolate should weigh one-fourth the amount of the melted chocolate. Never add blemished (untempered) chunks to the melted chocolate, or you will achieve the opposite of what is desired. For tempering chocolate, it is essential to use a thermometer that registers temperatures within a range of 80°F. to 130°F.

Working with the Chocolate Melt and temper more chocolate than you think you'll need, unless you plan to use it all at one time. The more chocolate in the bowl, the slower it will cool and the longer you'll be able to work with it before it needs rewarming. Leftover chocolate is reusable. If the chocolate becomes thick during use, place it in the microwave and heat it about 10 seconds; or place it in a warm water bath. Do not allow the temperature of the chocolate to exceed 90°F. (88°F. for milk and white chocolates), or you will have to retemper it (following directions in Step 2 below).

Chocolate is forgiving; if at first you don't succeed, melt your mistakes and try again.

The Recipe

To temper chocolate, follow this technique. The amount of chocolate used can vary, as long as you maintain the same ratio of chopped chocolate to chunk chocolate (1 lb. to 1/4 lb.).

2 lb. semisweet chocolate, coarsely chopped
8 oz. semisweet chocolate, in 1 or 2 pieces
(for tempering)

1 Microwave 2 lb. chopped chocolate on high about 2 minutes; stir. (Use medium power for milk and white chocolates, stirring more frequently to avoid overheating.) Microwave in increasingly shorter increments, stirring after each interval, until chocolate is nearly melted. Stir gently to complete the melt.

2 Submerge 8 oz. of the chocolate chunks in melted chocolate. Stir gently but thoroughly until temperature reaches a maximum of 90°F. (88°F. for milk and white chocolates). Remove partially melted chunks of chocolate. The chocolate is now ready to be tested.

3 Smear a thin chocolate sample on waxed paper and refrigerate about 2 minutes. If it appears firm and evenly glossy, it is ready to use. If it feels tacky and streaks appear on the surface, place the chocolate chunks back in the bowl and cool about 2°F. more. When chocolate is in temper, cool the chocolate chunks on waxed paper in the refrigerator until dry, about 10 minutes. Store at room temperature for future use.

Chocolate Heart Candies

Chocolate Heart Candies

Molding chocolate is a magical experience no matter how many times you do it. Since tempered chocolate contracts as it cools, the pieces release easily and mirror the surface of the cavity. Molds should be clean, dry, scratch-free and at room temperature. If you use multiple molds, you won't have to wait for the chocolate in one mold to set up before you can refill it. To make these candies, use three plastic heart-shaped molds with 18 (1¼-inch) cavities per mold.

1 lb. milk chocolate, coarsely
  chopped
Scant ¼ teaspoon orange
  oil
4 oz. milk chocolate, in
  1 or 2 pieces
Gold dust, if desired

1 Melt 1 lb. chocolate and orange oil in medium bowl. Stir until smooth. Temper using 4 oz. chocolate.

2 Using pastry bag or heavy resealable plastic bag with corner cut off or teaspoon, fill heart-shaped cavities of molds almost to rims with chocolate. Tap bottom of molds several times on work surface as they are filled to release air bubbles.

3 Refrigerate 15 minutes or until bottoms of molds appear frosted and chocolate is set. Invert onto waxed paper, flexing sides or tapping back of molds to release chocolate. If chocolate resists, refrigerate an additional 5 minutes. If desired, brush each heart lightly with gold dust.

4 Spread remaining chocolate on waxed paper. Refrigerate until set; store in airtight container.

About 54 hearts

PER HEART: 35 calories, 2 g total fat (1.5 g saturated fat), .5 g protein, 4 g carbohydrate, 0 mg cholesterol, 5 mg sodium, 0 g fiber

Chocolate Types

Unsweetened (bitter) chocolate, also known as chocolate liquor, is derived from processed cocoa beans. It contains nothing more than cocoa butter and cocoa solids. By law, chocolate liquor must be an ingredient in any product labeled "chocolate" (except white chocolate). Here's a review of various chocolates and how they can be used in making candy.

Couverture, which means "coating" or "covering," is a term used to identify cocoa butter-rich chocolates of the highest quality. They are very fluid when melted and have an appealing mellow flavor. The word couverture probably won't appear on the wrapper, but the price of a chocolate often distinguishes it from chocolates of lesser quality. Couverture is especially recommended for dipping truffles in a thin coating of chocolate, molding thin hollow shells or using as an ingredient in confectionery and baking recipes. Examples include Callebaut, Carma, Del Rey, Lindt, Peter's, Scharffen Berger and Valrhona chocolates.

Chocolate chips contain less cocoa butter than most bars of chocolate. They are formulated to hold their shape in baked goods without melting. When forced to melt, the chocolate is thick and muddy. Chocolate chips should never be used for dipping.

Extra bittersweet and bittersweet chocolate bars tend to have a deeper chocolate flavor and are apt to be less sweet than those labeled semisweet. However, they all can be used interchangeably in most recipes. Use bittersweet chocolate to make truffle centers; to dip candy, fruit or cookies; and for molding.

Milk chocolate contains less unsweetened chocolate and more sugar than dark chocolate, plus butterfat and milk solids, so it is lighter in color, less intensely chocolate-flavored and very heat-sensitive. As an ingredient, it is rarely interchangeable with dark chocolate, but it can be used in candy recipes specifically formulated for it, and for molding and dipping.

Semisweet chocolate is probably the most common chocolate used for candy-making and baking. The amount of sugar it contains is not regulated, however, so what may be semisweet to one manufacturer may be bittersweet to another. Use it as an ingredient in candy recipes, and for molding and dipping.

White chocolate is an ivory-colored, cocoa-butter-based coating that is similar in composition to milk chocolate, except for the absence of chocolate liquor. It, too, is very heat-sensitive and should be melted with care. Use it as an ingredient in recipes specifically formulated for white chocolate, and for molding and dipping. Do not confuse it with white confectionery coating, which does not contain cocoa butter.

White Chocolate Heart-Shaped Bark

Chocolate bark is one of the most practical uses for leftover tempered chocolate. There are no set rules for making it. Simply combine any amount of chocolate with chopped or whole roasted nuts, cut-up dried fruit, dry cereal or anything else that is crispy or chewy. This white chocolate bark is studded, rather than mixed, with a variety of tasty morsels; it would be equally delicious made with dark or milk chocolate.

- 1 lb. white chocolate, coarsely chopped
- 4 oz. white chocolate, in 1 or 2 pieces
- ¼ cup dried cherries
- ¼ cup chopped dried apricots
- ¼ cup chopped pistachios

1 With pen or pencil, draw 6 (5-inch) hearts on parchment or waxed paper. Place on large baking sheet, drawing side down; secure with tape.

2 Melt 1 lb. chocolate in medium bowl. Stir until smooth. Temper using 4 oz. chocolate.

3 Using drawing as guide, spread chocolate into heart shapes about ¼ inch thick. Immediately sprinkle with cherries, apricots and nuts, pressing lightly to secure them to chocolate.

4 Refrigerate 20 minutes or until set. Using metal offset spatula, remove chocolate hearts from paper. To serve, break into pieces.

6 hearts

PER PIECE: 435 calories, 24 g total fat (13 g saturated fat), 6 g protein, 52 g carbohydrate, 15 mg cholesterol, 65 mg sodium, 1 g fiber

Elaine González is the author of *The Art of Chocolate* (Chronicle).

White Chocolate Heart-Shaped Bark

Blackberry Meringue Bars

The Bar Scene

Luscious fruits strut their stuff atop buttery crusts in the season's best bars.

Recipes by George Geary

With fresh fruits at their peak flavors, it's time to head to the bar. Bar cookie, that is. Ripe peaches, blackberries, apricots and more pair elegantly and easily with buttery, melt-in-your-mouth crusts. The fruit flavors intensify as the bars bake, creating a pleasing contrast of tastes and textures.

For the busy cook, bar cookies have huge appeal. They're quicker to make than several batches of cookies, and they're versatile. Depending on how you present them, they can go from picnic (cut into brownie-sized squares) to tea time (dainty diamond-shaped bars) to dessert (served in bigger squares with a dollop of whipped cream).

Summer's fresh fruit awaits. Pick some up and start baking.

Blackberry Meringue Bars

This bar features three layers of heavenly flavor: a delicious almond-studded crust, an intense fresh blackberry center and a fluffy meringue topping.

CRUST
- 2 cups all-purpose flour
- 2/3 cup finely chopped sliced almonds
- 2/3 cup sugar
- 1 cup unsalted butter, softened

TOPPING
- 2 cups fresh blackberries
- 4 egg whites
- 1 teaspoon lemon juice
- 1/3 cup sugar
- 3/4 cup sliced almonds

1 Heat oven to 350°F. Line 13x9-inch pan with foil so that foil hangs over edges. Cut 13x9-inch piece of parchment paper; place over foil in bottom of pan.
2 In large bowl, beat all crust ingredients at medium-low speed until dough forms. Press into bottom of pan. Prick dough all over with fork. Bake 25 to 30 minutes or until pale brown.
3 Place blackberries in food processor or blender; process until pureed. Spread pureed blackberries evenly over crust.
4 In large bowl, beat egg whites and lemon juice at medium-high speed 1 to 1 1/2 minutes or until soft peaks form. Sprinkle 1/3 cup sugar over egg whites; beat 2 to 3 minutes or until stiff peaks form. Gently spread meringue over pureed blackberries; sprinkle with 3/4 cup sliced almonds. Bake 10 to 12 minutes or until top is light golden brown.
5 Cool completely. Remove bars by lifting foil ends. Slide bars with parchment paper liner onto cutting board. Cut into 36 pieces.

36 bars

PER BAR: 125 calories, 7.5 g total fat (3.5 g saturated fat), 2 g protein, 13 g carbohydrate, 15 mg cholesterol, 5 mg sodium, 1 g fiber

Apricot-Coconut Squares

Picture a rich, decadent nut pie filling, then add plenty of fresh apricots and flakes of coconut, and you have the sweet, tasty topping for these delectable bars.

- 2 1/3 cups all-purpose flour, divided
- 1 cup unsalted butter, softened
- 1/2 cup sugar
- 2 eggs
- 1 cup packed dark brown sugar
- 1/2 teaspoon baking powder
- 1/4 teaspoon salt
- 1 teaspoon vanilla
- 1 teaspoon lemon juice
- 1 1/2 cups chopped fresh apricots
- 1 cup chopped walnuts
- 3/4 cup flaked coconut

1 Heat oven to 350°F. Line 13x9-inch pan with foil so that foil hangs over edges. Cut 13x9-inch piece of parchment paper; place over foil in bottom of pan.
2 In large bowl, beat 2 cups of the flour, butter and sugar at medium speed until dough forms. Press into bottom of pan. Prick dough all over with fork. Bake 20 to 25 minutes or until pale brown.
3 Meanwhile, in same large bowl, beat eggs at medium-low speed until blended. Beat in brown sugar, remaining 1/3 cup flour, baking powder, salt, vanilla and lemon juice. Scrape down sides of bowl. Fold in chopped apricots, walnuts and coconut. Spread over crust.
4 Bake 18 to 20 minutes or until filling is set. Cool completely. Remove bars by lifting foil ends. Slide bars with parchment paper liner onto cutting board. Cut into 36 pieces.

36 bars

PER BAR: 150 calories, 8.5 g total fat (4.5 g saturated fat), 2 g protein, 17 g carbohydrate, 25 mg cholesterol, 30 mg sodium, 1 g fiber cutting board. Cut into 36 pieces. Store in refrigerator.

36 bars

PER BAR: 165 calories, 9.5 g total fat (5 g saturated fat), 2.5 g protein, 18 g carbohydrate, 50 mg cholesterol, 40 mg sodium, 1 g fiber

Chocolate-Raspberry-Pistachio Bars

These beautiful confections showcase whole fresh raspberries layered between a fudgy chocolate base and crumbled chocolate topping.

  2¼ cups all-purpose flour
  ⅔ cup chopped pistachios, divided
  ½ cup sugar
  ½ cup packed brown sugar
  ⅓ cup unsweetened cocoa
  1 teaspoon baking powder
  1 cup unsalted butter, cut up, softened
  1½ cups fresh raspberries
  2 oz. semisweet chocolate, coarsely chopped
  ⅛ teaspoon vegetable oil

1 Heat oven to 350°F. Line 13x9-inch pan with foil so that foil hangs over edges. Cut 13x9-inch piece of parchment paper; place over foil in bottom of pan.
2 In large bowl, stir together flour, ⅓ cup of the pistachios, sugar, brown sugar, cocoa and baking powder. With pastry blender or 2 knives, cut in butter until mixture resembles coarse crumbs. Reserve 1¼ cups of the mixture.
3 Press remaining mixture into pan. Arrange raspberries over crust. Sprinkle reserved 1¼ cups flour mixture around raspberries; sprinkle with remaining ⅓ cup pistachios. Press mixture down lightly.
4 Bake 20 to 25 minutes or until toothpick inserted in center comes out clean. Cool completely.
5 Place chocolate and oil in microwave-safe dish. Microwave on high 30 to 50 seconds, stirring once. Drizzle chocolate over cooled bars. Refrigerate until chocolate is set. Remove bars by lifting foil ends. Slide

Peach Frangipane Bars

Peach Frangipane Bars

Almond paste provides a heady backdrop for peaches in these rich bars. Use firm peaches because they soften a bit in baking. These bars are best made the day they will be served.

CRUST
  2½ cups all-purpose flour
  ¼ cup sugar
  ½ teaspoon salt
  1 cup unsalted butter, chilled, cut up
  2 egg yolks
  3 tablespoons cold water
TOPPING
  1 (7.5-oz.) pkg. almond paste
  ¾ cup sugar
  6 tablespoons unsalted butter, cut up, softened
  3 eggs
  1 teaspoon vanilla
  ¾ cup all-purpose flour
  3 firm but ripe medium peaches

1 Line 13x9-inch pan with foil so that foil hangs over edges. Cut 13x9-inch piece of parchment paper; place over foil in bottom of pan.
2 In food processor, combine 2½ cups flour, ¼ cup sugar and salt; pulse to mix. Add butter; pulse until mixture resembles coarse crumbs.
3 In small bowl, whisk together egg yolks and water. Add to flour mixture; pulse until dough forms. Cover and refrigerate 20 minutes or until firm.
4 Meanwhile, heat oven to 350°F. Press dough into bottom of pan. Prick dough all over with fork. Bake 25 to 30 minutes or until pale brown.
5 In food processor, combine almond paste and ¾ cup sugar; pulse until blended. Add 6 tablespoons butter, eggs and vanilla; pulse until well mixed. Add ¾ cup flour; pulse until combined. Pour over crust.
6 Cut each peach into 12 slices. Place slices in 6 rows of 6 slices each over almond paste mixture. Bake 40 to 45 minutes or until light brown and firm in center. Cool completely. Remove bars by lifting foil ends. Slide bars with parchment paper liner onto

Lemon-Macadamia Shortbread Bars

bars with parchment paper liner onto cutting board. Cut into 36 pieces. Store in refrigerator.

36 bars

PER BAR: 120 calories, 7 g total fat (3.5 g saturated fat), 1.5 g protein, 14.5 g carbohydrate, 15 mg cholesterol, 15 mg sodium, 1 g fiber

Lemon-Macadamia Shortbread Bars

This updated lemon bar, with its zingy lemon filling, was a favorite with testers. The shortbread base is enhanced with buttery macadamia nuts.

CRUST
- 1 cup roasted salted macadamia nuts
- ¾ cup sugar
- 2 cups all-purpose flour
- 1 cup unsalted butter, cut up, softened
- 1 tablespoon grated lemon peel

FILLING
- 6 egg yolks
- 6 tablespoons sugar
- 6 tablespoons fresh lemon juice
- ¼ cup unsalted butter, cut up, softened
- 1 teaspoon grated lemon peel
- ¼ cup chopped macadamia nuts

1 Heat oven to 350°F. Line 13x9-inch pan with foil so that foil hangs over edges. Cut 13x9-inch piece of parchment paper; place over foil in bottom of pan.

2 Place 1 cup macadamia nuts and ¾ cup sugar in food processor; pulse until nuts are finely ground. Add flour, butter and lemon peel; pulse until mixture is blended (dough will not form). Spread mixture in pan; press evenly to form crust. Prick dough all over with fork. Bake 20 to 25 minutes or until pale brown. Cool completely.

3 In heavy medium saucepan, whisk together egg yolks and 6 tablespoons sugar; whisk in lemon juice. Cook over medium heat 4 to 5 minutes or until thickened and temperature reaches 160°F. Remove from heat; whisk in ¼ cup butter and 1 teaspoon lemon peel. Place in small bowl; press plastic wrap directly on surface. Cool to room temperature; spread over crust. Sprinkle with ¼ cup macadamia nuts. Refrigerate 1 hour or until firm.

4 Remove bars by lifting foil ends. Slide bars with parchment paper liner onto cutting board. Cut into 36 pieces. Store in refrigerator.

36 bars

PER BAR: 145 calories, 10 g total fat (4.5 g saturated fat), 1.5 g protein, 12.5 g carbohydrate, 55 mg cholesterol, 5 mg sodium, .5 g fiber

George Geary is the author of *The Best 125 Cheesecake Recipes* (Robert Rose Publishers).

Recipe Index

This index lists every recipe in *The Best of Cooking Pleasures — New Creations*. If you're looking for a specific recipe but can't recall the exact name, turn to the General Index that starts on page 152. You can look up the recipe there by ingredient(s), and find what you're looking for.

General Index

There are several ways to use this helpful index. First — you can find recipes by name. If you don't know a recipe's specific name but recall a main ingredient used, look under that heading and all the related recipes will be listed; scan for the recipe you want. If you have an ingredient in mind and want to find a great recipe for it, look under that ingredient heading as well to find a list of recipes to choose from. Finally — you can use this general index to find a summary of the recipes in each chapter of the book (starters & appetizers, soups, salads & sides, main dishes and desserts).

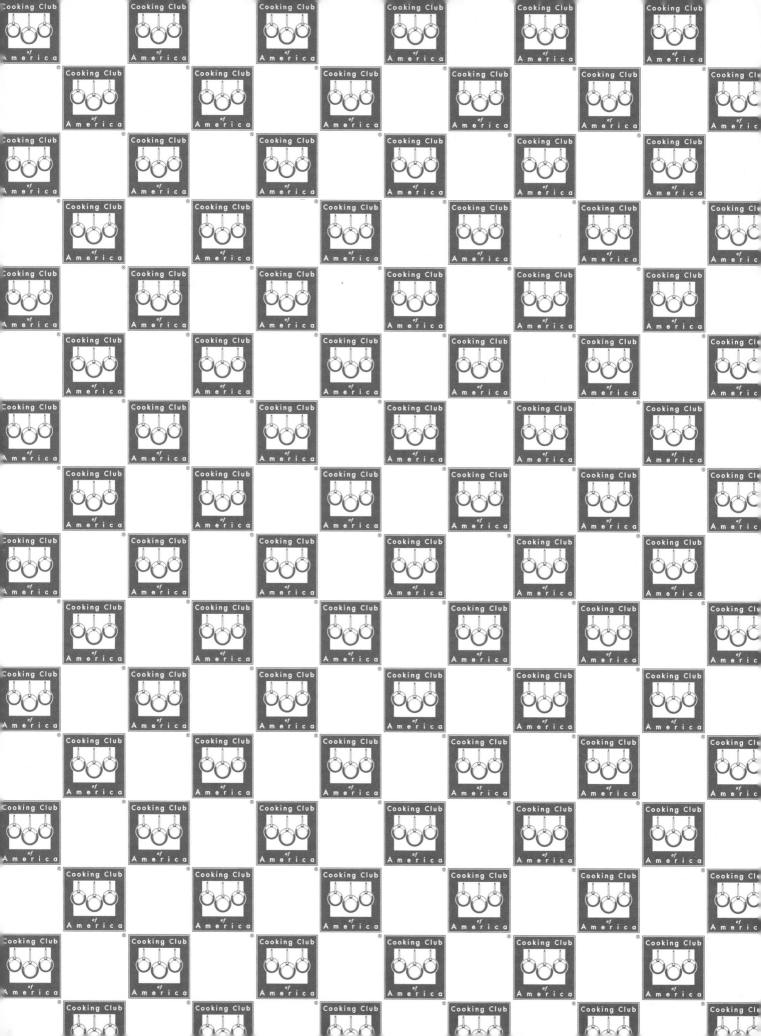